Thinking Is Child's Play

Evelyn Sharp

Thinking Is Child's Play

foreword by Patrick Suppes
DIRECTOR, INSTITUTE FOR MATHEMATICAL STUDIES
IN THE SOCIAL SCIENCES, STANFORD UNIVERSITY

E. P. DUTTON & CO., INC.   NEW YORK

Contents

5

More Difficult Games

foreword

Miss Sharp has written a useful and valuable book for all parents of young children. In Part One she provides a survey of current research about children's thinking, and in Part Two she uses this research to suggest a large number of games that may be played with children. These games will be fun for both parents and children. I do emphasize that the games should be thought of as games—they are not meant to be used by parents to attempt a professional evaluation of the cognitive development of their children, nor do they constitute a kind of homemade intelligence test. Playing the games with children will give parents insight into how children think and will also contribute, in ways we do not yet fully understand, to the children's own thinking processes.

Miss Sharp's book is bound to bring pleasure to many, old and young alike.

Patrick Suppes
DIRECTOR,
INSTITUTE FOR MATHEMATICAL STUDIES
IN THE SOCIAL SCIENCES,
STANFORD UNIVERSITY

Part One

chapter one

Children bring to their first day of school a wide variety of learning and of inhibition against learning. Beginners are very unequal, even those from families with the same cultural and economic background. To a large extent, they differ because they have had different experiences in their preschool years—a mountain of small day-to-day experiences that either stimulate mental growth or ignore it.

How can you help your child come to the opening of his school career in a position of advantage rather than disadvantage? The answer hinges on another question: What makes for success in schoolwork?

It used to be that the most effective tool a child could have was a good memory. Now, as a result of recent widespread changes in the school curriculum, the emphasis is on ideas, understanding, and insight. He is asked to analyze, to com-

11

pare, to draw conclusions—in short, to *think* instead of merely to memorize.

Let me make it clear that by "school" I mean the point at which the formal academic curriculum begins—that is, the first grade. Valuable as nursery school and kindergarten are in teaching children how to get along with others and adjust to the group, they are not the subject of this book. It is mental development that I am talking about.

The belief in a fixed intelligence that unfolds at its own sweet rate and in its own good time until it reaches a predetermined level is now largely discredited. A child's experiences play an important role in the development of his mind. Learning specialists no longer think that in the area of mental growth we can only sit and wait, the way we wait for a child's permanent teeth to replace his baby ones. If a child is not ready for learning, we can help him to become ready.

It is the experiences of the early years that are the powerful and indelible ones. Estimates of the percentage of an adult's intelligence that is formed before the age of six vary, but they are all high. By the time a child enters school, the groundwork of his education has already been laid, for better or worse. You have more influence on the development of your child's mind than any teacher ever will.

Starting from scratch, children have to build up, out of their own direct experiences, such concepts as quantity, distance, size, number, and space. Ideas that seem obvious to us are obvious only because we have gone through a protracted period of development. They are by no means obvious to a small child. Like an astronaut flung into orbit, he must orient himself in a world strange to him.

To help your child develop his powers of thinking, you need to understand how a child thinks, so that you can meet him on the level where he is. Listen—really pay attention —to what he says, and you can get a clue. Children's misconceptions often provide a peek inside their minds.

For example, take this incident: One Saturday morning a family's television set went blooey just a few minutes before time for Captain Kangaroo. Under pressure, Daddy, who hadn't dressed or shaved yet, hastily threw on an old torn sweater and a pair of dilapidated pants and took his little girl over to a neighbor's house so that she could see the program on their set. As they were standing on the porch, ringing the doorbell, the four-year-old said, "Get behind me, Daddy, so they can't see you."

Why did she think Daddy would be concealed if he stood behind her? For one thing, little children aren't aware that other people see things from a viewpoint different from their own. *She* couldn't see him when he was behind her; therefore he was hidden. For another, their thinking contains many contradictions, which don't seem to bother them. Although she undoubtedly knew that Daddy was much bigger than she was, she didn't carry that thought through to the conclusion that he would show, even if she stood in front.

The whole subject of children's thinking is a fascinating one. How do their minds work? Exactly what takes place when they learn? By what private logic do they reach conclusions perfectly reasonable to them but illogical to us?

Much exciting research is going on in an effort to find answers to these questions. Foremost is the work of Jean Piaget, the Swiss psychologist who pioneered the field and whose theories have had an unparalleled impact on education, especially in Europe. He has written (in French) over twenty-five books and 150 articles that are a gold mine of ideas about the development of a child's intellect.

About half the books and a few of the articles have been translated into English, but his style of writing and highly technical vocabulary make him a very difficult author to read in any language.

Following Piaget's lead, there has been a surge of research in a number of countries, including the United States. Reports of these findings, too, are often so hedged about with a thicket of professional jargon that they are inaccessible to the nonspecialist.

It would be of enormous help to you as a parent to know the discoveries that have been made so far. Although final answers have not been reached, much of significance has already been uncovered. You need to know these things now, while your children are little. My purpose in Part I is to bring you in everyday, informal language some of the researchers' findings that will be most useful to you.

Part II contains practical suggestions for some brain-sharpening games that you can play with your preschool-age child. Each one calls for the exercise of logical reasoning, and includes activity with real objects, which are better for the purpose than pictures or words. They are designed to provide experiences of a kind that will help a preschooler develop his rational powers, which are the essence of the ability to think.

chapter two

Piaget has been preeminent in his field for so long that he inspires a sort of awe. When he steps into his lecture room at the University of Geneva, carrying his battered briefcase, the chattering students fall silent as in the presence of an Einstein or a Toscanini.

He is now in his seventies, rather bald on top, with hair like a ring of white fur. Walking right to the desk, he begins to lecture in French, plunging immediately into very technical and difficult material.

On his desk there is a stack of students' identification booklets, part of the university's record-keeping system. Every student must get the signature of each of his professors, attesting that he is enrolled in such and such a course. As he talks, Piaget (probably from long habit) signs the booklets one by one, never breaking his flow of words. Such is the absorption in his lecture that neither he nor his students pay any attention to what his hands are doing, but at the end of class the booklets, which had been piled on the left, are all stacked on the right, duly signed.

Piaget usually gives only one class at the university proper—most of the Piagetian courses there are taught by his assistant, Bärbel Inhelder, a very pretty woman who appears to be in her forties. Much of Piaget's work is at the Institute for the Sciences of Education, which is affiliated with the university, and is housed in one of the buildings of the old League of Nations. Psychology students first attend the university a year or two and then go to the Institute for more advanced courses. The students fall roughly into three groups—those who are studying to become psychologists, those who are studying to become teachers, and a smaller number who plan to become doctors.

Piaget has spent a lifetime working with young children— he gained fame in the field before he was thirty. In a series of classic experiments, he formulated his original and brilliant theory of the stage-by-stage development of a child's mind. At the time, the impact of his developmental psychology was felt a great deal more in Europe than in America, but in the last few years he has been rediscovered, so to speak, and we are now in the midst of a sort of Piaget boom.

He began with observations of the babyhood of his own children—a son, Laurent, and two daughters, Jacqueline and Lucienne. He played with them the way any parent does, but at the same time he kept a meticulously detailed record of what they did—a record that is one of our richest sources of knowledge of a baby's mental development.

Here are some examples: When Laurent was ten months and sixteen days old, Piaget placed a big red cushion in front of the baby and laid his own watch on it. Laurent reached for the watch, but it was too far away. Then he grabbed the cushion and pulled it toward him until he could get the watch.

To test him, Papa Piaget complicated the game by using two cushions, one behind the other, with the rear cushion turned diagonally (like a baseball diamond) and partially lapping over the front one. He put his watch on the farthest corner of the diagonal cushion.

Laurent pulled the nearer cushion toward him, as before. Nothing happened—the watch didn't move. Then he discovered the place where the two cushions overlapped. Reaching partway across the first one, he grabbed the corner of the second cushion and pulled it over the first until he could get the watch. To Piaget, such behavior is a distinguishing mark of intelligence because it shows intention—the deliberate use of an instrument to reach a goal.

Jacqueline, at one year, four months, and three days, was playing with a little neighbor boy about the same age. He threw a temper tantrum—screaming, stamping his feet, and shaking the playpen bars. Jacqueline, a good-natured child, looked on wide-eyed—she had never seen anybody act like that before.

The next day, when her mother put her in the playpen, she screamed, stamped her feet, and shook the bars. To Piaget, the interesting point was that her imitation came, not at the time, but a day later—proof that she was reproducing the scene from memory and giving evidence of growing mental powers.

He played little games of hide-and-seek with his children, writing down precise observations of the conditions under which they could or could not find a hidden object. While ten-month-old Jacqueline watched, he hid her toy parrot under one side of the mattress she was sitting on. She found it with ease. Then he hid the parrot under the other side of the mattress, but Jacqueline hunted for it in the same place where she had successfully found it before, although she had plainly seen him hide it elsewhere.

The next developmental step came when she would always search in the place where she saw him hide the object, provided it was visible to her during the actual act of hiding, but not if it was invisible. For example, when she was eighteen months old she was sitting on a small green rug, playing with a potato by putting it into an empty box and taking it out again. Papa Piaget hid the potato in the box; then, slipping the box under the rug for an instant, he secretly dumped the potato and brought out only the box. When he asked Jacqueline to find the potato, she searched in the box, looked at Papa, looked at the rug. Puzzled, she tried the box again. It never occurred to her to look under the rug, because she hadn't actually seen Piaget put the potato there—it was concealed by the box.

An older child would have inferred that if the potato wasn't in the box, it must be under the rug. One month and twenty days later, in a similar situation where Piaget concealed a coin in his hand, put his hand under a coverlet, and then withdrew it, Jacqueline looked first in his hand. No coin. She then immediately searched under the coverlet, and found it—a neat, if elementary, piece of reasoning.

In his work at the Institute, much of it with four- to seven-year-olds, Piaget was the same papa-experimenter. He would set out a few familiar objects—perhaps a tray of beads or some clay—and give the child a little task to perform with them. Making use of his natural rapport with children, he asked questions not only about the objects, but, more importantly, other questions aimed at revealing the mental processes by which the child arrived at an answer. He followed the child's thought wherever it seemed to be going, varying the procedure according to the response.

Afterward he wrote down his observations, including a verbatim report of everything that was said. He analyzed these written accounts, then arranged them into categories according to the concept being investigated and the children's responses.

Piaget found that at each stage of development, children had a certain characteristic way of acting and thinking. He grouped these stages into four major periods, giving rough approximations of the age levels of each.

The first period (birth to one and a half or two years old) he called sensory-motor. Babies cannot think of an object they don't see at the moment. With them it is literally out of sight, out of mind. Put a handkerchief over a toy that a baby is reaching for, and he stops and pulls back his hand. It does not occur to him to lift up the handkerchief and look for the toy—he seems to think it has simply vanished.

Babies don't perceive objects the way we do. Piaget thinks that to a baby an object looks like a picture, appearing and disappearing. Not until near the end of the first year does a child develop the concept of the permanent character of objects—that is, that an object exists independently, even when it is hidden from sight.

The knowledge that things haven't gone away just because he can no longer see them is a landmark in the process of a baby's mental growth, and, as such, is incorporated in tests given by professionals. Dangle a small, attractive object (maybe a tiny doll) in front of a baby; then, while he is watching, put the doll under an overturned cup. A baby who has passed this milestone will lift up the cup and find the doll.

At first the concept of permanent objects is hazy and limited. A striking example of this mental pattern was exhibited by a cousin of the Piaget children—Gérard, a little boy thirteen months old. He was playing with a ball, dropping it on the floor and scrambling after it. When it rolled under an armchair, he looked under the chair and fished it out. The next time, it rolled under a fringed sofa. He made a halfhearted attempt to reach the ball, but the sofa was too large and deep, and the fringe obstructed his view. So he went to the chair and searched under it, although he had plainly seen the ball roll under the sofa. Piaget conjectured that to the child the ball was still a series of images appearing in different places and that these images were not yet completely fused into one separate and distinct ball, with an independent existence of its own.

During the sensory-motor period a child's actions, which at first were completely accidental and aimless, begin to show intention. Like Laurent, pulling the cushion toward him so he could reach the watch, children learn the relationship between means and end. They push a barrier aside in order to get a toy or they take a stick and poke the toy closer.

The threshold into the next period is marked by development of the concept of representation. The most obvious example is the use of words to stand for physical objects and actions. When a child learns to talk (that is, to put words together to mean something), you have a very strong sign that he has passed through the sensory-motor stage.

The second period, which Piaget observed in children up to about six and a half or seven years of age, he calls the preoperational. By "operations" he means complex mental acts that children in this stage are not yet capable of—hence the "pre." The latter part of this period is possibly the age most thoroughly researched by Piaget. It is especially important to us because it is the time of the preschooler.

At this stage a child judges size and other physical characteristics entirely by appearances, even though reason would show the truth to be otherwise. Pour all the milk from a tall glass into a shallow bowl—do it right before the child's eyes without spilling a drop—and he still is apt to think there is now a different quantity of milk than before. Children don't reason, as we would, that because nothing was added or taken away there must still be the same amount. If it looks like more, they think the quantity has actually increased.

When two changes take place at the same time, children tend to center their attention on only one, ignoring the other. One of Piaget's most famous experiments went like this: He made a ball of clay, and asked the child to make another one the same size—just as big and with just the same amount of clay. When the child was satisfied that the two balls were alike, Piaget took one and rolled it into an elongated sausage shape while the child watched. Was there now more clay in the sausage, less, or the same amount as in the ball? Piaget found that children in the preoperational stage usually said that there was more, because the sausage was longer.

They think this because they have not yet developed the concept of conservation of quantity. As with the milk, they do not understand that the amount can stay the same when the appearance is altered. Their judgment is based on how the thing looks to them; and, since they can't think simultaneously about the changes in width and length, their answers depend on whichever dimension has caught their attention (most often, length).

Conservation is one of the key points in Piaget's theory. Until they have developed this mental tool, children come to some strange conclusions—strange to us, that is. From a child's point of view they are perfectly logical.

In an experiment designed as a test for the conservation of length, Piaget laid two identical sticks side by side, with their end points aligned. (Children at this age tend to judge comparative length by looking at the end points of the objects.) He asked the child if the sticks were the same length, and the child said they were. Then Piaget moved one stick a little to the side, like this:

A child who was still a nonconserver would say that one stick was now longer "because it is ahead of the other one." He couldn't mentally hang on to the property of length, which remained unchanged while the stick was being moved.

This concept is of great importance educationally. Obviously, it is useless to expect children to understand anything about measurement as long as they think the length of an object changes every time it is moved to a different position. This would affect not only the object being measured but also the measuring rod itself. It would be like trying to use an elastic ruler.

Even more important educationally is the conservation

of number. Piaget was interested in studying what we call "number readiness," not arithmetic. We adults take for granted certain underlying facts about numbers—for example, that the number of objects in a group remains the same even if they are arranged in a different way. Little children don't comprehend this, as Piaget clearly demonstrated.

In a typical experiment he set out a row of cups and a basket of eggs. He asked the child to put one egg in each cup. Were there the same number of eggs as cups? The child said Yes. Then Piaget took all the eggs out of the cups and put them in a bunch, leaving the row of cups as it was. Now were there the same number of eggs as cups? The child said there were more cups.

In the preoperational stage children don't take into account the gaps between objects, but judge by the overall appearance. Eight objects spread out over a wide space seem to them to be more than eight objects clustered together in a small space. They do not yet understand that eightness is preserved throughout all changes in arrangement. Until they develop this concept, it is plain that children cannot really grasp the meaning of number, although they may have memorized the number-names, and can recite them like a nursery rhyme.

Conservation of various attributes does not develop all at the same time. For example, a child may be a conserver of length while still a nonconserver of number. The test for conservation of any characteristic is always the same. Confront the child with a situation where there is a conflict between logic and the optical illusion of appearance. Logic does not win the battle all at once. It must fight its way step by step against the compelling and, to the child, convincing testimony of his senses.

Piaget thinks that conservation hinges on the development of the concept of reversibility. In the realm of thought, for every action there exists another action that undoes it. The milk may be poured back into the tall glass, the clay reshaped into a ball, the eggs put back in the cups. At the preoperational stage a child can't visualize such reversals because he is tied to the world of reality where, so often, what is done is done, once and for all.

Notice that one of the great achievements of the sensory-motor period was the development of the concept of the permanence of objects—the realization that an object does not dissolve into thin air if it is hidden away in a drawer. Similarly, the great achievement of the preoperational period is the development of the concept that certain characteristics of objects are enduring in the same way—the knowledge that such things as quantity and number do not magically change just because the appearance of the object is transformed.

There are other characteristics of the thinking of children in the preoperational stage. They are enmeshed in their own point of view—so much so that they are unaware that to a person on the other side of the room a chair, for example, looks different from the way it does to them. Piaget clearly showed this in an experiment where he put a scale model of three mountains on a table, and seated a child and a doll on opposite sides of the table, facing each other. He asked the child to choose from a series of photographs the one that pictured what the mountains would look like to the doll. Younger children consistently picked the photograph showing the mountains from their own side of the table.

They are also unable to take another's point of view figuratively speaking, either. In studying a child's use of language, Piaget kept a month-long record of everything two children said at the Maison des Petits, a kindergarten in Geneva where much of his experimental work was done.

The results fell into two categories: socialized speech where the child talked in order to communicate something to the listener, and egocentric speech where the child talked just to be talking, perhaps to himself or at least without regard for the listener—a sort of monologue. Almost half of what was said was egocentric speech.

A later study analyzing the speech of twenty children turned out the same way. Even when they tried to communicate, the children were often unsuccessful because they merely said aloud what was in their minds. They couldn't mentally put themselves in the listener's place and choose words that would convey their meaning to him.

The last step in the preoperational period is mastery of the inclusion relationship. Just as children tend to center their attention on one characteristic at a time (such as length), overlooking the others, they also can't think of the whole and its parts at the same time. To them, the whole is destroyed when it is split into parts. In an ingenious experiment Piaget would show the child a tray of wooden beads. Most of them were brown, but there were a few white ones mixed in. Then he asked which would be longer—a necklace made of all the brown beads or a necklace made of all the wooden beads? Surprisingly, most of the children said the brown beads.

This is not just a foolish mistake, as it might seem to us. The child understands that all the beads are wood and that some are painted brown and some white, but he can't reason about the whole (wooden beads) and a part (brown beads) at the same time. When he thinks about one, he forgets the other. Asked to compare the brown beads with something, since to him the whole is gone, he compares them with the only thing left—that is, the set of white beads. Obviously, there are more brown ones.

The third period (according to Piaget, from about seven to eleven years of age) he calls the period of concrete operations. At this stage, children are conservers of quantity and of number. They understand the relationship between the whole and its parts. They reason in a way that seems rational to us, but always about the real world around them. They do not yet know how to cope with abstract thinking. That comes in the fourth and final stage—the period of formal operations, which lasts from about eleven to fourteen or fifteen, and leads to adult reasoning. The adolescent can think not only about the reality he sees but also about the potential. He can look at a situation, ponder all the possibilities, and select the one that fits the case at hand.

The burning question is: Can the transition from one stage to the next be accelerated? According to Piaget, the order in which the periods occur is fixed, but a child's rate of progress through them is not. His mental growth depends on several factors only one of which—the maturation of the central nervous system—is built in. A child's experiences with his environment are a powerful factor, and Piagetian theory points out that this is a two-way street. Not only is experience assimilated into the child's mental structure but, at the same time, his mental structure is accommodated to the experience, and changed by it. An intellectually stimulating environment leads to faster development.

Piaget is often asked whether a child's progress from stage to stage can be speeded up. His answer is Yes. However, he is opposed to high-pressured, extreme acceleration. He feels that there is an optimal time for the development of each concept and that this optimal time depends on the individual.

Children do not pass from one stage of development to another all at once, like crossing the border into a different country. Rather, concepts are constructed, layer upon layer. The transition is gradual, and the boundary lines are blurred.

Of special importance to us in this book is the transition from Period Two to Period Three, which roughly coincides with the child's entry into school. If the first grader still thinks in a way characteristic of the preoperational stage—for instance, if he is still a nonconserver of number—he cannot really understand much of the schoolwork, and will resort to memorizing and parrotlike learning.

chapter three

Because what a preschooler soaks up from his environment plays such an important role in his mental growth and educational achievement, there is a lot of talk today about the "hidden curriculum" in the home. Most often, it is strongly slanted toward reading. In a great many homes the children are read to, taught the names of things, and in general given a wide variety of experiences that are enormously helpful to them later in learning to read.

Very few have an equally rich opportunity to absorb number ideas in the same way. In most cases the only step that has been consciously taken is to teach the child to count. And counting by rote—that is, reciting the names of the numbers in order—has little to do with meaning.

Children can be taught to count, but an understanding of number is something they must develop for themselves out of their own experiences. Number is a logical concept built up from the fusion of two prenumber ideas—classification and seriation (arranging in order). A true understanding of number depends first of all on the development of these two logical operations, which underlie all types of analytical thinking.

There are definite steps that parents can take to foster this development during the crucial years before a child is six. Here is the area of greatest opportunity for you to help your preschooler increase his thinking skill and to give him just as rich a background for analytical subjects like mathematics and science as you are probably already doing for reading.

Classification requires the ability to recognize likenesses and differences between objects and to group them accordingly. It is a natural outgrowth of children's attempts to make sense out of the world around them—the means by which objects of their world are identified.

As an intellectual skill, classification lies at the core of certain kinds of learning. It is essential for problem solving in a variety of fields—mathematics, science, social studies, and so on. Some such ability to find likenesses in diversity also underlies creative thinking.

A child's first experiences in classification should be with physical objects. Children live in a concrete world. They can use logic and reasoning in handling material things long before they can do so with verbal problems.

In 1959, Piaget and his associate, Bärbel Inhelder, devoted an entire book to classification and seriation. (There are also many references in Piaget's earlier works.) They found that a child's ability to classify progresses gradually through three phases.

If a typical three-year-old is asked to put all the red blocks together, he partially and momentarily understands this and starts by grouping several red blocks. Then he loses the idea and begins to make the whole thing into something—a house, perhaps, or a truck—using blocks of all colors. It takes experience for a child to see similarities between objects, and to gather them together on that basis alone.

When he has reached the second phase, he can put all the red blocks in one pile and all the nonred ones in another. He appears to be in command of the classification concept, but he really isn't. There is still one area of confusion that will show up if the objects he is working with have qualities that overlap. For example, in one of Piaget's experiments there were two red squares, two blue squares, and five blue circles. These objects can be classified either by shape or by color. This isn't hard—a child in the second phase can do it either way. The tricky part comes from the fact that whichever way he chooses, there is some overlapping. If he classifies according to shape, all the circles are blue, but so are some of the squares.

To Piaget's question Are all the blue ones circles? most children correctly said No, because there were some blue squares. But when the question was turned around to Are all the circles blue? they still said No, which was wrong this time. All the circles *are* blue.

Children at this level do not understand how, at one and the same time, *all* of one thing can be *some* of another. In the example above, the same five objects comprise all the circles but only some of the blues. Not until they grasp this idea, which Piaget found was usually between seven and eight, do they attain genuine classification skill.

Let me caution you about Piaget's ages, which were true for the Swiss children he worked with but may not fit precisely in this country. Many American researchers believe that classification and other intellectual skills depend as much on the kinds of experiences a child has had as they do on age. If he is provided with systematic experiences in classification, he may reach each level earlier.

Seriation calls for arranging objects in a series according to some specified order. Because this concept is based on comparison, it is harder for children than classification, where they have only to decide whether or not an object possesses the required characteristic—for instance, "Is it red?"

In a charming experiment Piaget set up two toy clotheslines and gave the child some paper-doll dresses, pants, and shirts, to hang on one line. Then he asked the child to pick matching paper-doll clothes from a pile on the table and hang them on the second line in the same order.

Children under three couldn't do it at all. At three or three and a half they could match the items—dress to dress, shirt to shirt—but couldn't put them on the line in the right order. Furthermore, they saw no difference between their line and the first one. They simply didn't understand the idea of a fixed order. Slightly older ones saw that the two lines were different, and tried to correct theirs but couldn't quite get the hang of it.

A more typical seriation task is to arrange a group of objects in order according to a certain characteristic, such as size. Piaget used ten dolls differing in height but alike in every other way. As in classification, he found that this skill developed through three phases.

Children under five succeeded only in constructing fragments of a series—isolated pairs here and there. Between five and six they could form the series by a trial-and-error process, picking a doll at random and comparing it to another, then to another, and so on. Around seven, a new technique

31

emerged. They looked for either the shortest or the tallest doll, started with it, and systematically built up the whole series.

The key to seriation lies in the knowledge that if Doll A is taller than Doll B, and Doll B is taller than Doll C, then Doll A is taller than Doll C. Little children don't understand this at first. They can correctly compare A and B, and also B and C, but they can't put the two facts together. Arranging a complete series is beyond them until they develop this logical concept.

Some children are fascinated with comparing things. I overheard a five-year-old boy talking to himself about two jars on the table in front of him. Pointing first to one and then the other, he said over and over: "This one is bigger; that one is smaller. This is bigger; that is smaller." Then, reversing his pointing: "This is smaller; that is bigger. This is smaller; that is bigger," finally ending with, "This is glink; that is glunk."

In addition to classification and seriation, another pre-number idea of importance is one-to-one correspondence, which is a primitive way of guaranteeing (without counting) that two groups each have the same number of objects in them. Before he develops this concept, a child's notions about number and quantity are all jumbled together into the one vague idea of amount.

Line up a row of large buttons (or ships or bottle caps) on a table and ask him to make another row with the same number of buttons as yours. Younger children tend to make a row whose end points roughly coincide with yours but which may contain more buttons because they are crowded together, or fewer because they are spread out. They believe the number is the same if the rows are the same length. Around the age of five or six, on the average, a child will probably think of using the familiar "one for you and one for me" method, and construct his row by laying one button opposite each of yours.

If there is a natural affinity between the objects in the two rows (say you have a row of saucers and he has cups), he is usually able to make the one-to-one correspondence at an earlier age than with miscellaneous objects. Psychologists call the cup-and-saucer kind "provoked correspondence."

A child is sure that the two rows contain the same number of objects as long as they are lined up one to one, but that conviction leaves him when you spread the objects in your row farther apart or put them closer together. He can make the one-to-one correspondence sooner than he can conserve it in the face of changing appearances. Not until he becomes a conserver of number, which Piaget placed at about six and a half to seven (see Chapter 2), does he grasp the essential idea of number—that is, that the number of objects in a group remains the same no matter how they are shuffled around.

Counting is surprisingly little help to nonconservers in determining whether two groups contain the same number of objects. In an experiment done by Piaget and his associates, they found that children would often count the objects in each row, getting seven both times, and still say that there were more in the longer row. Seven was just a name to them. It didn't convey the idea that the two sets had an equal number just because they were both named seven.

Don't let your child's ability to count mislead you into thinking that numbers mean the same thing to him that they do to you. Children are great mimics—they do what we do, but often without understanding. I would say that reciting the names of the numbers in order has about the same relation to mathematics that reciting the alphabet has to reading.

If arithmetic is imposed on a child before he has developed the necessary prenumber concepts, he merely memorizes, thus storing up trouble for the future. He may be trying to learn mathematical symbols before he has anything to symbolize. Many first graders fill out workbook exercises without really knowing what they are doing. This leads to dislike and fear of math which usually solidify between the ages of six and eight.

Development of a child's abilities to think and learn in logical patterns comes through experiences with physical objects. I can't emphasize enough how strongly the tide is running toward the use of manipulative materials. Children gain understanding not from the objects, nor from what we tell them about the objects, but from their own actions on the objects. Firsthand experience is the key. They are capable of a high order of logical reasoning if given materials that they understand.

chapter four

For the last ten years there has been a strong movement in England to incorporate Piaget's ideas into their schools on a large scale. At a time when the former rigid structure of the British educational system was changing, there was an opportunity to introduce new ways of thinking about how young children learn. Piaget's discoveries did much to shape the direction these innovations took, especially in the Infant Schools.

To me, the word "infant" connotes a baby in a crib, but the British don't use the term that way. Their infants are the five-, six-, and seven-year-olds who attend the Infant Schools, a traditional name for the first three years of primary school. In England, also traditionally, five is the age when compulsory education begins, and I don't mean kindergarten.

35

A typical room in an Infant School doesn't look like a classroom. It looks, as one visitor said, like a "laboratory of homemade material operated by children"—a neat capsule description.

What you see is a wide variety of articles grouped into work stations arranged on tables. There are bottles and jars in all shapes and sizes, and water to fill them with. There are scales and balances surrounded by things to weigh—acorns, conkers (horse chestnuts), washers, screws, rice, dried peas. Some tables have a great profusion of objects for classifying, matching in one-to-one correspondence, and counting —beads, buttons, drinking straws, pipe cleaners, marbles, shells, and so on. There are rulers and yardsticks, both marked and unmarked, for measuring everything the children can think of.

You will find some of the well-known commercially manufactured equipment, such as Cuisenaire rods, but the innovators in the English schools emphasize raw materials— sand, clay, string, paper, cardboard boxes, paint—which they think give the children greater freedom to explore than manufactured kits with built-in, predetermined routes to follow.

Besides all this, the typical room has an aquarium and some hamsters, a Wendy house (playhouse) big enough for six children to get into, a play store that uses real money, and a library alcove with a wide variety of storybooks, graded reading series, and reference books on different levels of difficulty.

The method of teaching is to present a problem to a small group gathered at one work station—usually a problem about something the children are already interested in. Materials for solving the problem are at hand, but nobody points this out or tells the children how to go about it. They are left free to devise their own solutions so they may experience the power and confidence that come from the ability to think for themselves.

Some of the children's methods are very ingenious. For instance, a group of five-year-olds found out how fast a tadpole grows by dipping it out of the aquarium with a spoon, then holding it down on a sheet of paper and drawing around it before they put it back in the water. They repeated this procedure every day. (That tadpole is never going to make it to frogdom.)

There are about thirty-five or forty children in a class, but because of the number and variety of activities going on at once, the group at any one work station is small—possibly only two or three. The emphasis is on individualized, informal teaching, which they believe is more suited to the nature of small children, who are insistently individual and active, than the traditional formal classroom organization.

The children are free to move around, talking to each other and to the teacher while they work. (Anyone who has watched little children has noticed that their natural pattern of learning is to talk about what they are doing while they are doing it.)

For more space they overflow into the hall, as when some six-and-a-half-year-olds used the floor to mark out the height of a nine-foot giant in a story they had just heard. Then the children took turns lying down beside the giant's measure to compare their heights to his.

The point of view of the innovators in the British Infant School is, in substance, this: Intellectual growth depends on two things—innate potential and stimulating environment. Readiness for developing a concept comes from biological maturation coupled with massive quantities of experience involving a full range of materials to which the concept applies.

The Infant Schools attempt to supply the stimulating environment and the quantities of experience. Leading up to the concept of conservation of quantity, the children pour water or sand back and forth from one to another of a great variety of containers—observing, comparing. They mold clay into all manner of different shapes. With an eye to the concept of conservation of number, they sort and count acorns, buttons, pennies, or whatever interests them. For spatial concepts they build models of houses and buses out of cardboard boxes, cover them with paper cut to fit the surfaces, and paint the whole thing—a process that calls for much handling of shapes and viewing them from all angles.

Some Infant Schools use Piagetian-type conservation tasks as tests to chart a child's progress in learning concepts. Such tests are based on the teacher's observations of what a child does with the physical materials and what he says about them; therefore they must be given individually.

Bulletin Number 1, written by the British Schools Council for the Curriculum and Examinations, includes some conservation tests, and, purely on an experimental basis, suggests the following procedure for those children who show they have not yet developed the concept in question: Give twenty minutes a day of planned experience for six days, then retest. If no progress is shown, wait three months before repeating the twenty-minute-a-day, six-day sessions of further experiences, and then test again.

The purpose of the three-month wait is to allow time for biological maturation. Research done elsewhere (H. Beilin, *Journal of Experimental Child Psychology,* 1965) showed that experiences are most helpful when the child is in the transitional stage between conservation and nonconservation—that is, he is on the threshold but has not yet developed the concept.

Educators in other countries have also used Piagetian

tasks as tests. The next step appears to be the construction of a new intelligence scale based on Piaget's research.

In many quarters there is dissatisfaction with present IQ tests for young children. Among other things, they have been criticized for being too dependent on verbal ability, for being too broad and too superficial, for not really measuring what they purport to measure, and for not probing deeply enough into mental processes. Piaget's theory that a child's intelligence develops in sequential stages, each marked by characteristic and identifiable ways of thinking, would seem to lend itself to the construction of a scale for measuring mental maturity.

Piaget himself has never undertaken the construction of a standardized intelligence test, but at least two major efforts by others are currently under way. One is in Canada under the direction of Father Adrien Pinard at the University of Montreal, using children from two to twelve years old. The second is by Piaget's colleague Bärbel Inhelder and others at the University of Geneva who are working with children aged four to twelve.

Both include about twenty-five to thirty Piagetian tasks drawn from his research into children's concepts of such things as quantity, number, space, movement, time, and velocity. Both use Piaget's technique of individual interview-observation, but standardize it so that the procedure is the same for every child instead of varying the questions according to the child's responses as Piaget did.

In the United States, the University of California's Science Curriculum Improvement Studies program, headed by Robert Karplus, is an example of the application of Piaget's theories to educational practice. They have worked out materials and methods of teaching science in kindergarten and elementary school that make use of his discoveries about children's ways of thinking.

The project has made some demonstration movies showing the Piagetian concepts of conservation and classification. The conservation film is an eye-opener. It shows three kindergarten children and Karplus sitting around a low table with two half-filled glasses of colored water on it—one red, one yellow. The children all agree that both glasses have the same amount of water in them.

Then Karplus puts out a tall narrow jar and tells one kindergartener to pour all the yellow water into it. When the child does, the water naturally stands higher in the narrow container than it did in the original glass. Even teachers accustomed to five- and six-year-olds are surprised to hear the children all say that there is now more yellow water than red. To adults, of course, it is obvious that there is exactly the same amount of yellow water as there was before it was poured.

Nonconservers don't reason that way. They judge the amount of liquid by a single feature—something that they can point to. Here (as is usually the case) it is the height of the water.

When Karplus, a university physicist, began to teach little children, he found out that one of the most important things he could do was to listen to what they had to say, paying attention not only to the words but also to the ideas behind them. His technique is to present the child with some strategically chosen object, give him time to investigate its properties by looking, squeezing, poking, lifting, rubbing, pinching, and so on, then get him to talk about his observations.

Five- and six-year-olds are by nature manipulators of objects. Karplus feels that verbal definitions are not very satisfactory for the endeavors of science, and should generally be avoided.

Like the British Infant Schools, the California science

program emphasizes firsthand experiences with concrete objects. Kindergarteners sort paint chips and buttons. Equipped with paper bags, they go on an object walk outdoors, collecting leaves, pebbles, an occasional bird feather, and the like—all to be duly observed and classified later. Indoors, they play a game called "object-grabbag-relay" where each team lines up single file in front of its own bag of colored blocks. The children take turns drawing a block from the bag and trying to match it to one of seven other blocks spread out on the table. First graders investigate and classify metals, wood, powdered substances, liquids, gases, plastics, seeds, and plants.

Some of the worldwide interest in Piaget's work took the form of validation studies of his experiments, made by replacing his informal methods with more scientific techniques. The children were selected from a representative cross section; they were matched to control groups with similar backgrounds; complete data on the number of children taking part and other pertinent facts were recorded; and a statistical analysis was made of the results.

In general, these studies found a predictable sequence of stages of mental development agreeing with Piaget, but the children did not fit quite so neatly into the patterns. There was more latitude for individual differences, more variation attributable to factors other than chronological age, such as the child's social and economic background and his previous experiences. Neither did the age limits for the various stages of development exactly jibe with those for Piaget's Swiss children (some of them observed twenty years ago).

There is also a difference of opinion about the part that vocabulary plays in the experiments. Children are often vague about the precise meaning of words like "longer," "length," "more than," "number," and so on. By avoiding such words and substituting a nonverbal technique, some researchers found that responses characteristic of a certain stage could be elicited earlier than Piaget had suggested.

For example, two professors at the University of Alberta, Canada, repeated some of Piaget's experiments on the conservation of length, but with one important change. They used concrete models to convey to the child exactly what was meant by "longer" and "shorter" instead of depending on his interpretation of the words. They set up three calipers with rods inserted in the openings. In one model the rod was too long to fit between the prongs of the calipers, and stuck out; in another it was too short, and left an empty space on one side; in the third the rod exactly fitted into the opening.

Leaving the models set up for comparison, they gave the child another rod, and showed him how to apply his own calipers to it, then choose which of the three models showed a fit like his. When he could do that correctly four times in succession, demonstrating that he understood how to use the calipers, they went on to one or another of the classic experiments.

Suppose it was the one with two sticks described on page 22. First they put out two rods of equal length, and the child applied the calipers to each, showing that the fit was the same for both. Then they moved one rod to the left, as in the diagram on page 22, and asked him how the calipers would fit now *if* he were to try them on again, "Like this, or like this, or like this?" pointing to the three models. Results of the Canadian study showed that about 60 percent of the children between five and six years old were conservers of length, which is one and a half to two years younger than Piaget's age for development of this concept.

chapter five

A thumbnail résumé of typically American characteristics among this country's researchers would probably point out that they are optimistic, that their methods are apt to be electronic and computerized, and that accounts of their experiments are replete with statistics. The American to whom Piaget himself applied the word "optimist" is Jerome Bruner, psychologist and director of Harvard's Center for Cognitive Studies.

Piaget was referring to Bruner's widely publicized belief that enormous possibilities can be opened up by enriching a child's environment. The difference of opinion between the two men on this point is one of degree. Bruner views a child's mental growth as a series of stairsteps, each one containing certain capacities that must develop as a prerequisite to the next higher step. Some environments can slow the sequence down; others move it along faster. It is on the

43

amount of change that can be brought about by the environment that he differs with Piaget. Piaget thinks the amount is moderate; Bruner thinks it is great.

Bruner not only stresses the part played by environment, he wants to do something about it. Where Piaget is an observer whose work has been directed toward finding out what it is that children understand at each stage of development, many of Bruner's efforts are aimed at increasing their understanding, and accelerating their movement up the staircase.

Bruner does not think the sequence of steps is very clearly linked to age, although he agrees that a marked change in thinking takes place when the child learns to talk, another occurs at between five and seven years, and a third at the beginning of adolescence. These points roughly coincide with Piaget's ages for the transition from stage to stage. (See Chapter 2.)

At Harvard he has used variations of Piaget's methods in some of his own work. For example, he repeated the Piagetian experiment on conservation of liquid quantity, but he put a low screen between the glasses and the children (aged four to seven), so that only the tops of the glasses were visible.

First he showed the children a glass half full of colored water and next to it an empty glass that was wider. Then, behind the screen, he poured all the water from one into the other. The children could see the water going into the top of the wide glass, but not the level to which it rose. When he asked if there was still the same amount to drink, half the four-year-olds and almost all the others said it was the same.

Next, he removed the screen and again asked the same question. The four-year-olds changed their minds when they actually saw the lower water level in the wide glass, and said the amounts were different. The older children stuck to their first answer. The four-year-olds were taken in by appearances—they were perception-bound. The older ones did not fall for the illusion any more than we do when we see a magician pull a rabbit out of an empty hat. They (and we) have developed a sort of immunity to the spell cast by appearances.

What is the nature of this immunity and where does it come from? Bruner's explanation involves his theory that humans have three systems for processing and representing information: one is through action, one is by means of visual images, and one uses symbols. Adults can easily switch from one to another of these three or use them in combination, as the situation requires. Children can't. The symbolic system is the most sophisticated and hardest to handle; therefore little children depend on the first two.

In the experiment, they couldn't see much of the glasses, so the ordinarily dominant visual image was blocked out. Therefore, according to Bruner, they did the problem in their heads, using some symbolic system to represent the unseen water.

His interpretation is that when the screen was removed, the four-year-olds' weak symbolic system was overwhelmed by the impact of what they saw. The older children were immune because they had developed a symbolic system strong enough to withstand the visual illusion.

Symbols may be of many kinds. Basically, they are a sort of code or shortcut way of representing things. The most common, all-purpose symbolism is language.

It is here, on the role of language in thinking, that Bruner and Piaget part company. Piaget regards language and thought as two different but closely related systems. His view is that, although language is an aid, it is not in itself sufficient to bring about the mental operations that are the essence of systematic thought. He attributes the child's attainment of conservation to the growth of logic, not to his developing skill with language.

Bruner's experiment was an effort to find out what factors lead to the development of conservation. The procedure described above was part of a series of similar experiences in pouring liquid from one container to another. Sometimes the second glass was taller as well as wider; sometimes it was only one or the other; sometimes it was identical to the first glass. In one version the children, in advance of the pouring, pointed to the level they thought the water would reach. In another they made marks on the screen to show their estimate of the water level in the hidden glass.

Both before and after the series Bruner gave the children the classic Piagetian task to test for conservation. The four-year-olds, all of whom were nonconservers to start with, stayed the same, but the others made decided improvements. Conservation among five-year-olds jumped from 20 percent up to 70 percent. Almost all the sixes and sevens became conservers, compared to half when the series began.

However, when a screening technique was tried in the ball-of-clay experiment for conservation of solids, it proved ineffective. Bruner thinks it was because the children saw too much. The experimenter concealed the clay under two bowls turned upside down. First, he showed the child the two identical balls. Next, he put one ball under a bowl while he shaped the other into something of the child's own choosing—a hot dog or a pencil, for instance. When the object was finished, he put it under the other bowl. Then he asked the child if the two amounts of clay were the same.

This experiment was with a different group of children— eighty-one first graders, all nonconservers—and screening was only one of the techniques employed. The others were manipulation (the child shaped the clay) and labeling, where the experimenter used the child's own descriptive words—"fattest," "most spread out"—to talk to him about every step.

The overall pattern of the investigation was this: The eighty-one children were divided into eight groups. In each group the experimenter used a different technique or combination of techniques. However, in every case the clay shape was transformed four times, and the children judged the comparative amounts each time.

By far the most effective method turned out to be a combination of manipulation and labeling. While the child patted and rolled the clay, the experimenter encouraged him to talk about what was happening with questions like, "Is it as fat as the other one yet?" About 80 percent of this group learned conservation.

Bruner's explanation goes back to his theory of the three systems of representation. The children were at an age when the visual image is dominant. Only by teaming together are the other two systems—actions (manipulation) and symbols (labeling)—strong enough to win out against the powerful influence of appearances.

How can Bruner's findings help you? These points are notable:

1. The success of the combination of manipulation and labeling correlates well with the methods of the British Infant Schools.

2. Although the children in Bruner's clay experiment were chosen because they were nonconservers, they were all in the age range when conservation normally appears. His results jibe with findings by other psychologists that experiences are most effective when the child is close to developing conservation but has not yet done so. (See Chapter 4.)

3. The experiences were given individually—one child at a time.

Some American researchers use electronic equipment to

help solve one of the big problems in experimental work—the accumulation of enough data on which to base a valid conclusion. In contrast to Piaget's patient questioning, spread out over a period of forty years, they hope to speed up the process by utilizing computers and other machines and to amass large quantities of data in a comparatively short time.

One of the best known of the electronic researchers is Stanford's Patrick Suppes, director of the university's Institute for Mathematical Studies in the Social Sciences. Youthful-looking, dynamic, brilliant, he spearheaded the construction of a million-dollar computer-based laboratory at the Institute in 1964, financed by a grant from the Carnegie Corporation of New York.

The laboratory has two uses—first, for experimental work in pursuit of an answer to the universal question How do children learn? Second, for developing new teaching techniques that apply modern technology to actual elementary-school classrooms.

The nerve center of the laboratory is a fast medium-sized computer with six individual terminal stations hooked into it. A child seated at a terminal is looking at a marvel of technical ingenuity. Each station has a cathode-ray tube, like a small television screen where drawings of such things as dogs, turtles, toy trucks, squares and triangles appear—or possibly letters, numbers, words, and math problems, depending on the child's age. At the same time a taped voice gives instructions.

The younger children (kindergarten and first graders) answer by touching the screen with a light-projecting pen. For them, the voice might begin by saying, "Touch the dog." Older ones can peck out their answers on a typewriter keyboard attached to the bottom of the screen. Either way, the computer instantly gets the message and records not only the child's response but also his reaction time, down to the fraction of a second.

Every station also has a screen on which microfilms can be projected. The equivalent of a 512-page book may be encoded on microfilm, and the computer can come up with any desired part of any page in one second flat. Here, too, the children respond by touching the light-projecting pen to the screen.

One of Suppes' experiments of special interest to us was an investigation into children's ideas about certain geometric figures. The screen displayed a standard equal-sided geometric figure (triangle, square, etc.), and below it two variations of the same figure. Each child was asked to point to the bottom figure that he thought was most like the top one.

The variations involved only two factors—a change in size and a rotation of the figure so that it stood in a different position, something like this:

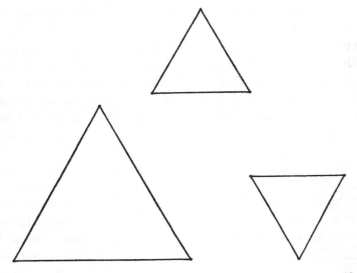

Note that the triangle on the bottom left is changed in size from the top one, but like it in every other way. The triangle on the bottom right is a replica of the top one, but turned so that it stands on its tip.

The experiment included many examples that were not so clear-cut as this—both bottom figures might be enlarged and turned around, but in differing degrees. In all, he used displays of sixty triangles and also similar diagrams of thirty-six squares and eighteen pentagons. They were run in two series in two separate sessions with the children.

He collected a large amount of data from California children of widely varying ages (nursery school three- and four-year-olds up to sixth graders) and with different cultural backgrounds. The results were surprising. First graders overwhelmingly ignored a difference in size, and matched to the standard triangle at the top the figure that was standing in the position most nearly resembling it. They saw little similarity between the figure that had been turned around and the model at the top. In other words, a change in size didn't prevent them from seeing similarity, but a rotated position did.

Among older children this tendency uniformly and significantly tapered off. It also dwindled on going down the age scale the other way—kindergarteners showed it less than first graders, nursery-school children less than kindergarteners. The youngest children were almost as apt to pick one figure as the other, showing no very marked preference. The tendency definitely peaked in the first grade. Why?

On a trip to Ghana in connection with the African Educational Program (a cooperative enterprise conducted by scientists and educators from America, England, and several African countries) Suppes tried a form of this same experiment. Ghanaian six-year-olds, many of whom came from families with a high rate of illiteracy, showed no such tendency. What is there about American culture that causes first graders to be very observant of changes in the position of a drawn figure, but to ignore changes in size?

Suppes conjectured that it is because first grade is the time when most American children begin reading. Part of learning to read is to become indifferent to changes in the size of letters, at the same time becoming sensitive to the way they are placed on the page. "A" and "ᴀ" mean the same, but "d" and "p" are two different symbols. The twenty-six letters of the alphabet are always shown in the same position —turning them around makes a different letter.

The fact that among preschoolers the tendency steadily rose with age seems to me to reflect the abundance of reading-readiness influences at work during these years. Quite aside from formal materials, children are steeped in experiences with such things as traffic signs ("No left turn," "Slow," etc.) and brand names on television commercials, which they usually learn to recognize early.

Suppes' finding has a very practical application in mathematics readiness—that is, make use of the prevalent orientation toward reading, and begin by presenting geometric shapes standing in a fixed position, as letters of the alphabet are.

We do this automatically with number symbols, but I, for one, didn't think about its application to geometric shapes until I read the results of Suppes' experiment. It gave me a clue as to why a little girl (five years, eight months) didn't recognize the triangles when she was trying to duplicate a pattern of cardboard shapes. I had laid out a row of colored squares, circles, and triangles and then given her a stack of similar cutout shapes. She went through them, one at a time, and matched the squares and circles to the pattern, but she skipped right over the triangles. To her, they didn't seem to match the model. I think, now, that it was because the triangles in her hand were turned around. (Squares aren't as easily disguised, and circles, of course, are the same whichever way they are turned.)

Suppes is convinced that clues to the secrets of the learning process should be sought in the classroom itself. In November, 1966, he and Richard Atkinson, Stanford psychologist, opened a second computer-based laboratory at Brentwood Elementary School in East Palo Alto. It is similar to the one at the Institute, but larger, with eighteen terminals in order to accommodate a whole class at once. Half of Brentwood's more than one hundred first graders took their mathematics lessons from the computer—the other half took computerized reading lessons. The next year the program was extended into the second grade.

The computer acts as a sort of mechanical tutor capable of handling many children at the same time, yet giving individualized instruction to each one. The math lessons (Suppes) and the reading lessons (Atkinson) were developed on four to six levels of difficulty. The first grader starts with basic material and is then quickly branched up or down according to how he does.

Within the lessons, each problem is prepared in depth so that what a child sees and hears next is tailored to fit his answer. The computer can come up with appropriate material depending not only on whether he is right or wrong but also on his particular type of error.

At the beginning of school the children first learn how to use the equipment—earphones, light pen, and so on. The next step for the younger ones is to familiarize them with words like "top," "bottom," "right," "left," "first," and "last" so that they can follow the spoken instructions. Maybe the voice says, "Put your light pen on the turtle shown at the top," or, "Touch the first toy truck." ("Right," "left," and "last" proved to be the hardest.) Instructions are kept to a minimum because the children get restless and their attention wanders if the voice talks for longer than ten seconds without giving them something to do.

When the child makes a correct response, the computer supplies what the psychologists call "reinforcement" by displaying a small star on the screen for one and a half seconds. When he is wrong, an "X" appears. Sometimes a drawing of a smiling face lets him know he is right—a sad face means that he isn't. If he has trouble in understanding, he can touch a "help box," and the voice explains while arrows show up on the screen like bouncing balls in the old sing-alongs. Children become surprisingly at ease with the machines—or maybe it isn't so surprising, in a world of television sets and electronic-eye supermarket doors that open by themselves.

While it might appear to be a far cry from the British Infant Schools' "laboratory of homemade material" to a computer-based laboratory for first and second graders, there is an underlying similarity. Both emphasize individual learning. They represent two approaches to the problem of providing a situation where the child's progress is not tied to the class. Suppes says that one of the best substantiated facts in psychology is the existence of significant individual differences in rate of learning.

There have always been children for whom learning was easy and children for whom it was hard. Cumulatively, the goal of researchers today is to find out exactly how the easy learners do it, and to share the secret with the others. Discoveries made so far are steps in that direction.

Part Two

The idea behind each of these games is based on the work of researchers, both here and abroad. After looking around the house and the supermarket, I used the materials I found there to devise some games for the home. None of them is meant to be mastered in the way a lesson is. They are play, but play with a purpose.

In most, the purpose is to give your child explicit firsthand experiences of a kind that will provoke thinking. Some are intended to give you an indication of the level of mental development your child has reached, in order to help you understand his way of reasoning as contrasted to an adult's.

The games are divided into two groups, based on difficulty. I don't want to peg them rigidly to a certain age—children who are exactly the same number of years old, to the fraction, may be at quite different points of development. For that matter, the term "preschooler" itself is rather flexible because the age at which children begin school is not uniform. The month they were born in makes a big difference. A child whose birthday falls near the last of September might start to school before he is quite six. On the other hand, one whose birthday is in December won't start until the following autumn in most places, which makes him close to seven.

In broad terms, the age range covered is from about four for the very simplest games up to about six and a half for the most difficult ones. I suggest that you start with the first group—if they prove to be too easy, go to the second group.

Here are a few pointers on the techniques of presenting the games:

1. Let your child think for himself. Give him plenty of time. If he doesn't succeed after several trials, it's all right to give him a hint, but never *tell* him the answer. Hints can be like stepping-stones laid out across a stream, but he has to jump from one to another by himself. If you carry him across, he has really learned nothing. Every solution that he works out for himself gives him confidence, and makes the next problem easier.

2. Let him perform for himself whatever actions are called for—pouring, sorting, and so on. Let him do it even if he spills things or seems to take a long time. Overlook such incidents. Always make the game a pleasant experience.

3. The wording I used in the games is meant only as a suggestion. Vary it to suit the situation—you are the best judge of whether your child understands what he is asked to do. However, where he is to compare two things and make a decision about them, be careful not to ask loaded questions—that is, questions phrased in such a way that they

influence his answer. Even your tone can give him a clue in such cases, so try to be as noncommittal as possible.

4. The games are less effective if continued too long at a time. Don't keep at it for over ten or fifteen minutes at the most—make the session even briefer for a four-year-old. Stop while your child is still interested and will want to play again another day.

Directions for Making Colored Cards

Some of these cards are used for a dozen or so of the classification and seriation games, so it's easier if you make them all at once while you have the materials out. The quickest way is to trim a deck of old playing cards into the required squares, triangles, and circles, but you can cut them out of thin cardboard if you prefer. You will also need one roll each of red, green, blue, and yellow plastic Scotch Tape, 3/4 inch wide. (See the tips on the next page before you start.)

Begin by trimming a 1/4-inch strip off the end of a card, to get rid of the curved corners. Now along the length of the card measure a distance equal to the width, and cut off the excess so that you have a square. If you are using plain cardboard, make it 2 1/4 inches on each side. Cover both the face and the back with tape. Make eight of these squares—two each of red, green, blue, and yellow.

Triangles are made the same way as squares, but with one additional step. After you have trimmed the card so that it is the same length as width, mark the midpoint of the top edge and connect this point with each of the two bottom corners to form a triangle. You will need five triangles—two red, one blue, one yellow, and one green.

To draw a circle, trace around a can or something similar.

The top of a jar of baby food just fits on a card. (I am not suggesting that you start these games while your child is still a baby—use little brother's baby-food jar.) Make five circles—two red, one blue, one yellow, and one green.

Tips: Use the low numbered cards—they have more white space. Fours make especially good triangles.

In the tape I used, blue was the most opaque, green the least so.

Make the red cards from the red suits. There is less tendency to show through.

Tape 1 1/2 inches wide works well, but costs twice as much. Save the cardboard cores from the rolls of tape. They can be used in one of the other games.

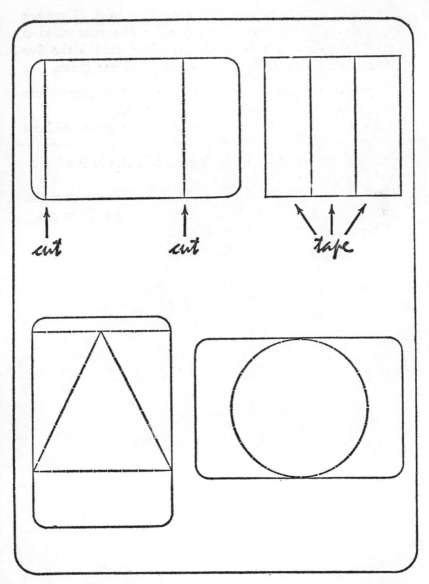

Beginning Games

game one

Purpose: To provide experience in classification by color.

Materials: The eight squares from the set of colored cards.

Spread the squares out in no particular order but with all of them plainly visible. Single out a red one.
"What color is this?"
"Can you point to another red one?"
"Put the two red ones together."
Repeat with each of the other colors. Then mix them all up again.
"Can you put the ones together that are alike?"

Comments: Children use color, shape, and size in classifying things around them. Color is the easiest of these three attributes, and the best place to start. Colors with decided and striking differences come first—subtle gradations of shade and hue should not be used until later.

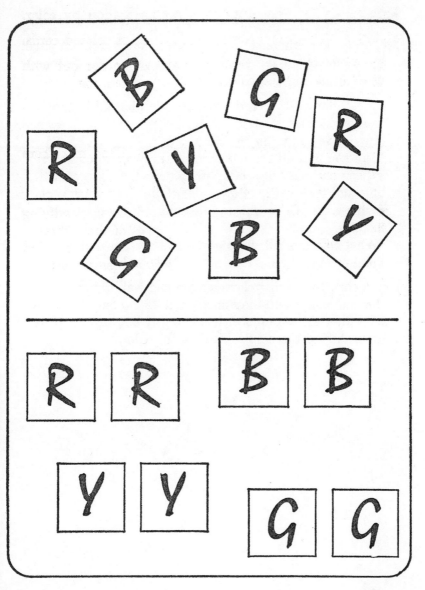

63

game two

Purpose: To provide experience in classification by color.

Materials: The whole set of eighteen colored cards. A small piece each of the same red, blue, and yellow plastic tape used in making the colored cards.

Spread out all the cards on one side of a fairly large working surface, such as a table or the floor. Stick a small cross of red tape on the other side.
"Can you find all the red cards and put them over here?"
When your child has successfully done that, repeat with blue and then with yellow (identifying each sorting place with a cross of the appropriate color), leaving each group in place.
"What color are all these cards that are left over?"
Point out that he has now sorted the whole set by color.

Comments: In the first classification game all the cards were the same shape and the same size, differing only in color. Here they differ in more than one way but are classified according to the single attribute of color.

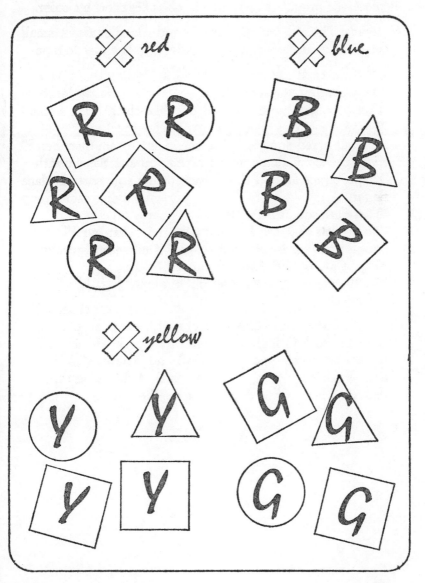

game three

Purpose: To provide experience in classification by shape.

Materials: The red squares, circles, and triangles from the set of colored cards.

Put the six red cards on the table, spreading them well apart. Single out a red circle.
"Can you find another round one like this?"
"These are circles. Put the two circles together."
Pick out a red square. "Can you point to another one that's the same shape as this?" As you say the word "shape," trace around the outside of the square with your finger.
"These are squares. Put the two squares together."
"These two that are left are triangles. They go together because they are the same shape." Again trace around the outside of the card as you say "shape."
Mix the cards up. "Can you put the ones together that are alike?"

Comments: It is important to begin with cards all the same color in order to highlight the difference in shape.
Use the words "square," "circle," and "triangle," but always point to the appropriate card at the same time so that the child is not dependent on the name.

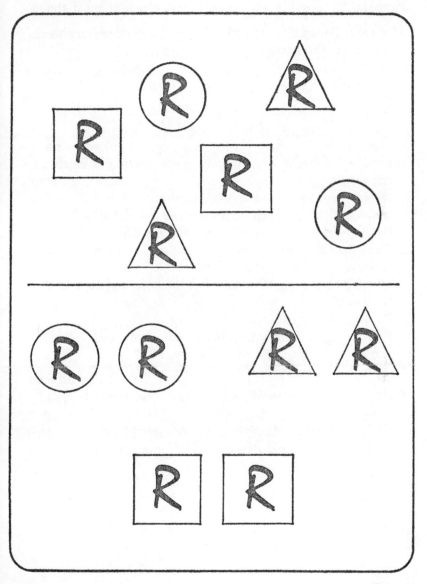

game four

Purpose: To provide experience in classification by shape.

Materials: A round white plate about nine or ten inches in
diameter. (May be paper, plastic, china or whatever
you have.)
The whole set of eighteen colored cards.

Spread out the cards and put the plate beside them.
"Can you find a card that's round like this plate?"
"Let's make Mr. Round Man with two round cards for
eyes and a round card for his nose and round cards for
his mouth."
As your child finds the cards, put them in the plate, using
green and blue for the eyes, yellow for the nose, and
overlap the two red circles for the mouth.
Take the cards out of the plate and mix them up again.
"Can you make Mr. Round Man?"
When he has done that, take out the nose and replace it
with a triangle.
"Is he still Mr. Round Man?"
Replace the mouth with three squares, curved around
the edge of the plate to make a smile.
"What is he now? Maybe Mr. Mixed-Up Man?"

Comments: If your child puts some of the wrong shapes in
the plate when he is trying to make Mr. Round Man, go
ahead and make Mr. Mixed-Up Man right away, using
his cards, but emphasize that this is not Mr. Round Man.

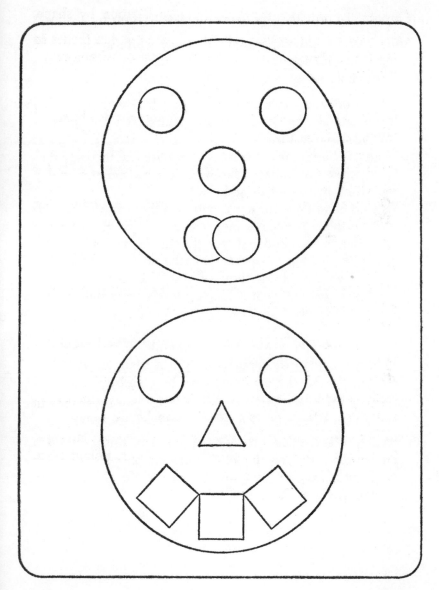

game five

Purpose: To provide experience in classification by shape.

Materials: A white paper napkin, or any white square about one foot on each side.
The whole set of eighteen colored cards.

Spread out the cards and the napkin beside them.
Trace around the edge of the napkin with your finger.
"What shape is this?"
"Can you find some cards that are square like this napkin?"
"Let's make Mr. Square Man with his eyes and nose and mouth all made out of squares."
As your child finds the cards and puts them on the napkin, arrange them to make a face, using the two blues for the eyes, the yellows and reds for the mouth, and stacking one green on top of another for the nose.
"Would he still be Mr. Square Man if I do this?"
Put a triangle on top of each mouth square so they look like snaggleteeth.
"Why not?"
"Could we make a Mr. Triangle Man?"
Fold the napkin diagonally to form a triangle. As the child picks out the cards, place a blue and a green triangle to form the eyes, a yellow one for the nose, and fit the two red triangles together to make the mouth.

Comments: The colors are not important in this game. We are concentrating on shape. The placing of colors that I used are merely suggestions—let your child change them around any way he wants to.

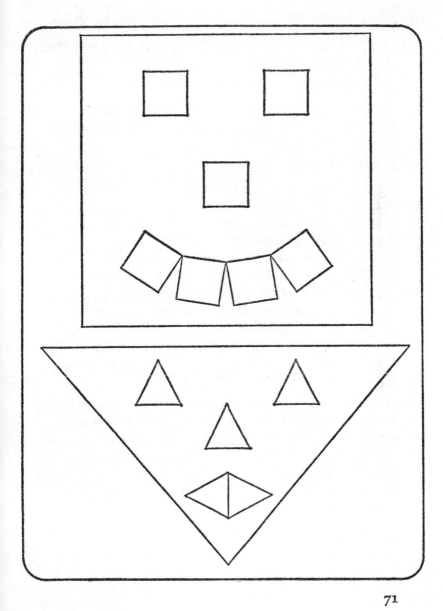

game six

Purpose: To provide experience in classification by shape.

Materials: A dozen objects chosen from the following three
categories, including at least two from each category:
1. rectangular—cereal boxes, Kleenex boxes, cake-mix
boxes, shoe boxes, and so on.
2. cylindrical—Quaker Oats boxes, Morton's Salt boxes,
some ice-cream containers, most canned foods (un-
opened), and so on.
3. spherical—balls.

Put the dozen objects on the floor in a random fashion.
Pick up a ball first.
"Can you find another ball?"
"Put all the balls together."
Take one of the rectangular boxes and call your child's
attention to the corners, letting him feel them.
"Can you find another box with corners like this one?"
Continue until all the rectangular boxes are grouped
together. The objects that are left are all cylinders. Show
him how they are alike in shape, especially the round
ends.
(Trace around the ends with your finger.)

Comments: Since we live in a three-dimensional world of
shapes, objects like these may be easier for your child to
recognize than flat shapes. Let him play with the objects
any way he wants to—children learn as much from
handling, lifting, and feeling as they do from seeing. Don't
try to teach him names like "cylinder" and "sphere."
Concentrate on recognition of the shapes.

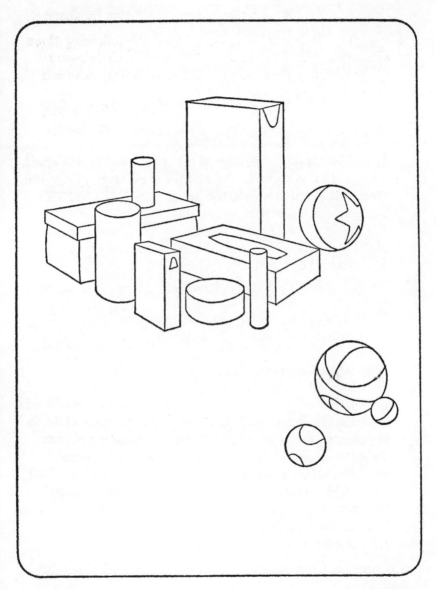

game seven

Purpose: To provide experience in recognizing order.

Materials: Three spools of thread in three distinctive colors, such as red, white, and green (or, if you prefer, three empty spools covered with the same tape you used to make the colored cards).
The cardboard tube from the center of a roll of paper towels.
A piece of string about a yard long.

Run the string through one of the spools, sliding the spool along until it is about in the middle of the string. Loop the string over and through the spool again, as shown in the diagram, so that it won't slip.
Do the same with the other two spools, spacing them about 1 1/4 inches on each side of the center spool.
Pull one end of the string through the cardboard tube far enough to bring the front spool up to but not inside the tube.
"Watch while I pull the spools inside the tube."
Be sure your child has a good look at the spools as they go in.
Stop when the spools are hidden from sight.
"If I keep on pulling, which spool do you think will come out first?"
"Pull the string and see." Let him pull until the first one appears, to see if he is right, but no farther.
Take the other end of the string and pull until the spools are hidden inside the tube again.
"Now which spool do you think will come out first if you pull this end of the string?"
"Pull it out and see."
Repeat with the spools in a different order.

Comments: Keep your hands over the ends of the tube

when you ask the questions. The first thing most children will do is to look inside and try to see what's coming. There is a more difficult version of this game (using the same materials) on page 140.

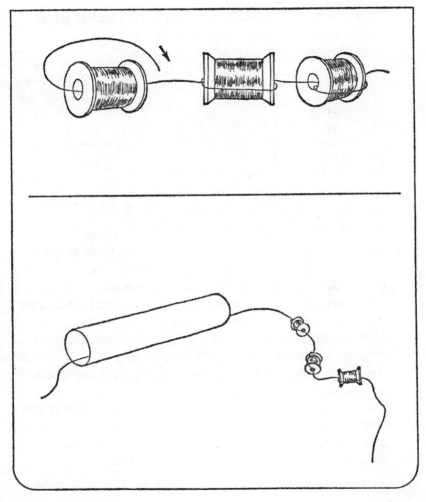

game eight

Purpose: To let you know if your child has reached the stage of mental development where he is a conserver of quantity. (See Chapter 2.)

Materials: A container of ready-to-bake biscuit.

Take out two biscuits. If they are too sticky to handle easily, sprinkle a little flour on them.

"Are these two the same size?" Let your child put one on top of the other to see for himself. When he is satisfied that they are the same, roll one of the biscuits between your palms to form a ball, pressing it securely together. (Let him do it if he wants to.)

"Does the ball have the same amount of dough as the other biscuit?"

"Would the ball be just as much to eat?"

Repeat with another pair of biscuits, but this time roll one into a hot dog shape instead of a ball. After the last question say, "Let's cook them and see."

Comments: Don't expect your four- or five-year-old to be a conserver, although he will probably enjoy the test, especially if he can eat the biscuit afterward. Try the experiment several times, a month or two apart. During the transitional period there is a sort of on-again off-again type of conservation when a child is sometimes a conserver, sometimes not. Don't try to teach him the fact that the ball still has the same quantity of dough as before. He might memorize the correct answer about the biscuit, but that does not mean that he would possess the concept of conservation of quantity in general. Instead, give him many opportunities to observe in similar situations.

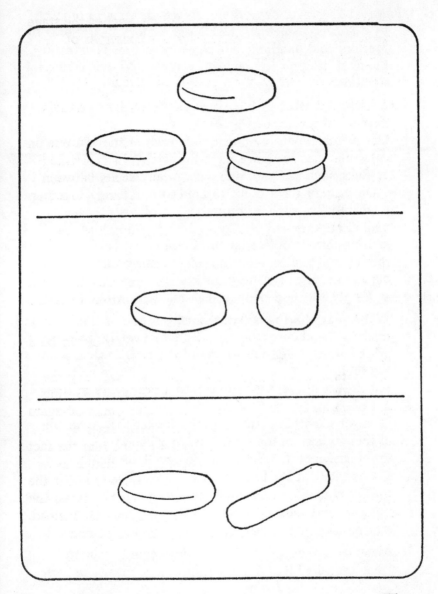

game nine

Purpose: To provide experience in classification of objects by a nonvisual method. (Children explore their world by touching and handling as well as by seeing. They make the most progress if a concept is presented in a variety of situations.)

Materials: A basket or box, such as a shoe box.
A small towel or scarf.
One matched pair of objects from each of the following categories (colors don't have to match):
1. Balls, such as Ping-Pong, golf, or any kind that are small enough for a child to hold in one hand.
2. Round lids such as those on jars of instant coffee, malted milk, or jelly.
3. Ring-shaped objects such as cardboard cores of the rolls of tape you covered the colored cards with, shower curtain rings, or plastic bracelets.
4. Empty salt and pepper shakers.

While your child is not watching, put one of the balls in the basket and cover the top with the towel. Line up the other ball, one lid, one ring, and the pepper shaker on the table.
Put the remaining three objects in a drawer, or at least out of sight.
"I've got something hidden in this basket that's like one of these things on the table. Put your hand under the towel, and feel it. Which one do you think it's like?"
Let him look at the four objects on the table, but not at the one concealed under the towel. Repeat with the lid, the ring, and the salt shaker, one at a time. Make sure that he does not see which object you put in the basket.

Comments: Piaget found that children could recognize what are called topological forms at a younger age than they could the geometric forms, what are more familiar to us. A ring is a topological form—its distinguishing feature is that it has a hole through it.

Piaget's experiments showed that, by using the sense of touch alone, children could tell an object with a hole through it from one without a hole when they were about three and a half, but it was several years later before they could differentiate between cardboard squares and triangles just by feeling them. (For visual recognition of topological figures, see the next game.)

game ten

Purpose: To let you know what stage of development your child has reached in recognizing and reproducing certain figures. It is not his artistic skill that we are testing, but his ability to distinguish the characteristics of each figure. Pay no attention to whether his drawings are lopsided, wobbly, messy, and so on. Look only for the identifying characteristic specified in parentheses in each case.

Materials: Several sheets of paper.
Two pencils or crayons.

Equip your child and yourself with paper and pencil.
1. "I'm going to draw something on my paper. Here's a cross. Can you draw a cross?"
(Does his drawing show two distinct lines?) Don't try to correct or criticize his drawing. Go on to the next figure.
2. Draw a freehand circle. Don't be finicky about your own drawings or try to be too accurate.
"Here's a circle. Can you draw one like it?"
(Does he draw a closed curved figure?)
3. "Here's a big circle with a little one inside it. Here's one with a little circle outside it."
(Do his drawings show that he recognizes the differences between the inside and the outside of the circle?)
4. "Now I'm going to draw a square. Can you draw a square?"
(Does his drawing show that he is thinking of straight lines rather than a curve? Does it have four sides?)
5. "Here's a triangle."
(Straight lines rather than a curve? Three sides?)
6. "Now a triangle inside a square. Can you draw that?"
(Look for two things. Is one figure inside the other?

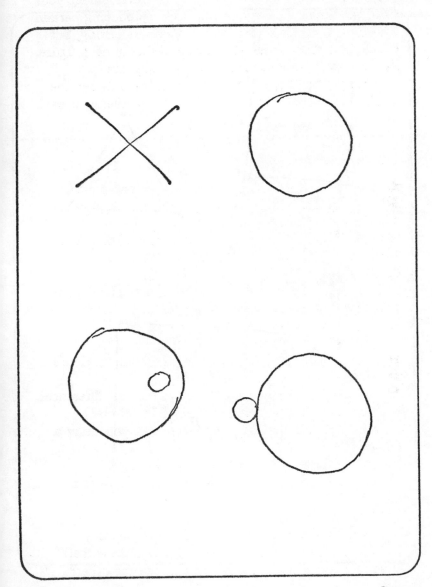

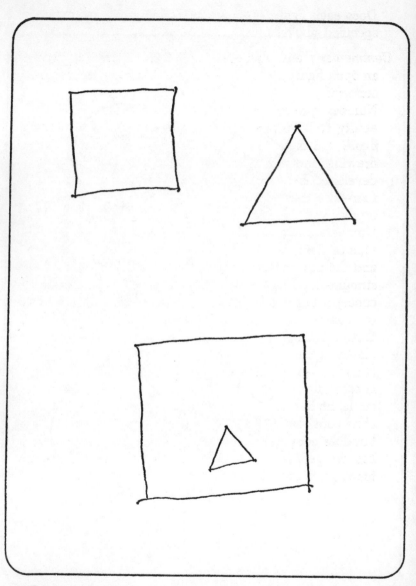

Does each figure show the identifying characteristics specified above?)

Comments: 1 and 2 test the ability to distinguish between an open figure and a closed figure. This is a topological concept.

Number 3 tests another topological concept—the ability to distinguish between the interior of a closed figure and the exterior. Piaget's observations of children's drawings indicated that topological concepts are usually developed between the ages of three and a half and four—also that geometric concepts are based on topological ones, and therefore develop later.

Numbers 4 and 5 illustrate certain geometrical concepts, such as the difference between curved and straight lines, and the number of sides and angles characteristic of each straight-sided figure. Children who have the topological concepts but not the geometric ones will make drawings of squares and triangles that are indistinguishable from their drawings of circles. They know that all three are closed figures, but that's all.

Number 6 is a combination of the two types of concepts. If a child's drawing looks like one circle inside another circle, he has developed only the topological relationships. If he consistently draws the square and triangle correctly, but does not place one inside the other, he (surprisingly) has the geometric concepts but not that particular topological one.

game eleven

Purpose: To provide experience in classification by size.

Materials: At least six pairs of objects that are alike in every way except size, such as:

A large and a small tube of the same brand of toothpaste. (The boxes they come in make an additional pair.)
A teaspoon and a tablespoon.
A large and a small box of the same brand of cereal.
A plate and a saucer or smaller plate of the same color or pattern (paper, plastic, or china).
Two sizes of cellulose sponges (same color).
A large and a small cake of the same brand of soap.
A regular and a miniature box of salt.

Spread the objects out in a random fashion. Pick up one of the boxes.
"Can you find another box that looks like this?"
"Are they exactly alike?"
"Which one is smaller?"
Repeat with two or three more pairs, lining the smaller objects up in one row and the larger in another.
"Can you sort the rest of these things the same way?"
When he has finished, mix the objects up again.
"Can you sort them this time by yourself?"

Comments: Of the three attributes most commonly used in classification (color, shape, and size), size is the hardest for children because it requires a comparison. No one thing is "larger" all by itself, but it can be red or square without reference to a second object.

game twelve

Purpose: To let you know if your child has reached the stage of mental development where he is a conserver of length. (See Chapter 2.)

Materials: Two pencils, equal in length. (The easiest way to be sure they are equal is to use unsharpened pencils.)

Place the pencils side by side with their end points aligned.
"Are these pencils the same length?"
Slide one about an inch to the left. "Are they the same length now?"
If he says No, ask, "Which one do you think is longer?"
Move the pencils so they are at right angles to each other, and repeat the questions.
Stand one pencil on end and repeat the questions.

Comments: In Piaget's experiments only about 12 1/2 percent of the children were conservers of length at the age of five. On the average, they were seven when they developed this concept. (See Chapter 2 for results obtained by other researchers, using a nonverbal technique.)
There is an optical illusion involved in some of these arrangements. When the pencils are placed at right angles, the vertical one does appear to be longer. Children are taken in by this illusion, but adults have learned to use logic in interpreting what they see.

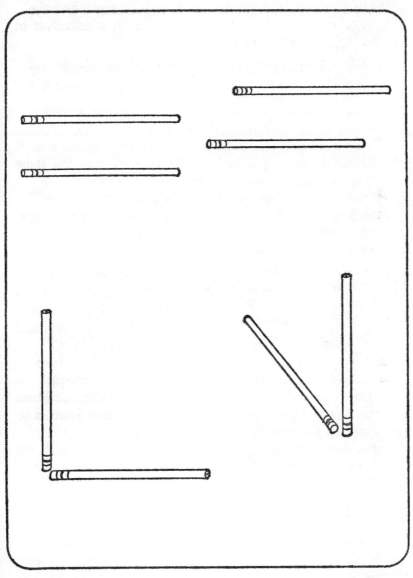

game thirteen

Purpose: To provide experience in duplicating a pattern.

Materials: The set of eighteen colored cards.

Spread out the cards on the table. Arrange five as in the top pattern shown in the diagram.

"Can you make a row exactly like mine?"

If your child can match the cards but gets them in the wrong order break the operation down into steps.

"Can you find a blue square and put it right below mine?"

"What comes next in my row?"

"Do you have a card like it?"

"Put your red circle next in your row."

And so on until he completes his row.

(Notice that there are only six pairs of duplicates in the set of cards—four pairs of squares, one pair of red circles, and one pair of red triangles. Be sure that your pattern is made from these cards so that your child has matching cards to choose from.)

Repeat with the second pattern as suggested in the diagram—this time see if he can do it entirely on his own.

Comments: Duplicating a pattern calls for the same abilities that Piaget tested in his experiment with the doll clothes hanging on two lines. (See Chapter 3.) He found that children younger than three had no concept of the problem at all. At three and a half they could match the items but were unable to get them in the right order.

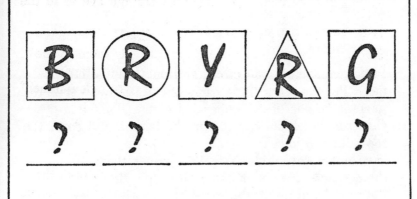

? ? ? ? ?
___ ___ ___ ___ ___

_____

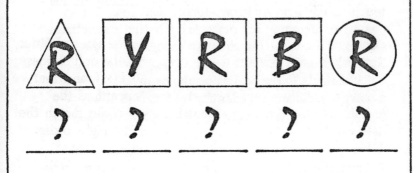

? ? ? ? ?
___ ___ ___ ___ ___

game fourteen

Purpose: To provide experience in classifying objects by a nonvisual method.

Materials: A basket or box, such as a shoe box.
A small towel or scarf.
Two squares, two circles, and two triangles from the set of colored cards.

Place one square, one circle, and one triangle on the table. Put the other three cards out of sight. To start the game, take one of the concealed cards (don't let your child see which one), put it in the basket, and cover the top with the towel.
"I've got a card hidden in this basket that's the same shape as one of these three on the table.
Put your hand under the towel and feel it. Which one do you think it is?"
Repeat with a different card in the basket.

Comments: Piaget's experiments showed that children are not able to identify geometric figures such as these by touch as early as they can topological figures (see comment for game on page 78). Of the geometrical shapes, the easiest for them to recognize is the circle. Kenneth Lovell, a British researcher, made similar (but not identical) findings. His results showed the circle to be as easy for children to identify by touch as the topological figures, with only the straight-sided geometric figures being harder.
A five-year-old that I played the game with said, "I felt all around like this." She put her fingers, held stiff, on the outside of the card and turned her hand around, feeling on all sides.

game fifteen

Purpose: To provide experience in classification according to negative information.

Materials: Nine of the colored cards—three squares, three circles and three triangles (a red, yellow, and blue in each shape).
A shallow box or tray of a size suitable to hold the cards.

Spread the cards out on the table with the box beside them.
"Can you find a card that is not red? Put it in the box."
"Is there another card that is not red?"
"Put all the cards that are not red in the box."
Spread the nine cards out on the table again.
"Can you find a card that is not a circle?"
"Put all the cards that are not circles in the box."
Spread the nine cards out on the table again.
"Can you find a card that is not red and not a circle?"
"Are there any others that are not red and not circles?"
"Put them in the box."
"What card is left on the table?"
Spread the nine cards out on the table again.
"Show me a card that is not blue and not a square."
Repeat with other combinations, both described negatively.
Switch to one positive and one negative description, such as, "Can you find a square that is not red?"
"Put all the blue cards that are not triangles in the box."

Comments: Watch for two kinds of mistakes. Possibly a circle is put in the box with the not-circles. Or perhaps everything in the box is classified correctly, but not all the cards are put in there that should be. If this happens, pick up the misplaced card and say something like, "Is this a card that is not red?" (or "not blue," "not square" or whatever category fits.)

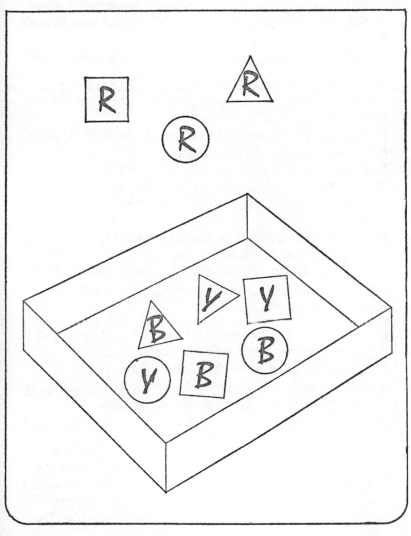

game sixteen

Purpose: To provide experience in classification according to "either . . . or" information.

Materials: Nine of the colored cards—three squares, three circles, and three triangles (a red, yellow, and blue in each shape).
A shallow box or tray of a size suitable to hold the cards.

Spread the cards out on the table with the box beside them. "Can you put all the cards that are either blue or yellow into the box?"
If this concept proves difficult (and it well may), break it down into steps. "All the blue cards belong in the box and all the yellow ones do, too." Pick up a yellow card. "Is this blue? . . . Is it yellow? . . . Then it goes in the box." Repeat with a red card, showing that it does not go in the box.
"Do you see any more cards that are either blue or yellow? Put them in the box, too."
When your child has found them all, spread the cards out again. "This time put all the cards that are either circles or triangles into the box."

Comments: Both this concept and the one in the preceding game are important in the formal study of logic. They are introduced informally, early in the grades, through operations with sets, a part of the math program. The diagram for this game is the same as for the preceding one.

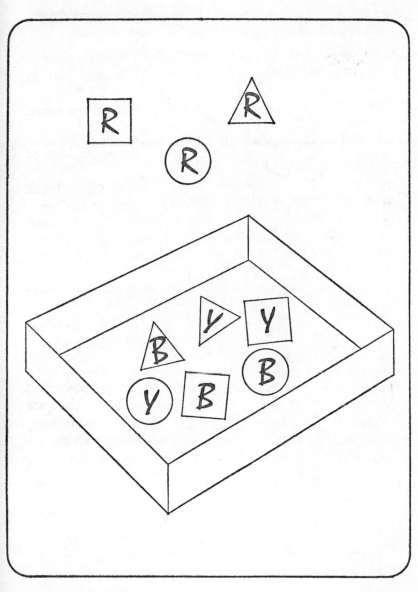

game seventeen

Purpose: To let you know if your child has reached the stage where he is a conserver of quantity. (See Chapter 2.)

Materials: Two identical, average-size glasses.
Two smaller glasses, such as juice glasses.
Two different colored liquids, such as tea and orange juice, two flavors of Kool-Aid or anything similar (carbonated beverages won't work).
A shallow bowl (glass or plastic clear enough to see through).

Fill one of the identical glasses about three-fourths full of tea and the other about three-fourths full of orange juice (or whatever liquids you're using).
Place them side by side on the table, making sure that both liquids come up to the same level in the glasses.
"Is there more to drink in my glass than in yours?"
"Suppose I pour my tea into these two little glasses." (Do so.) "Now does one of us have more to drink than the other?" Conservers will say No, that both are the same. They see right through the maneuver of pouring. If your child says Yes, ask him which one and why he thinks so. Pour the tea back into the original glass. "Is there the same amount in both glasses now, or is there more in one?"
"Suppose you pour your juice into this bowl." (Encourage him to do so.) "Do both of us still have the same amount to drink?"

Comments: Don't be surprised if your child is not yet a conserver of quantity—most four- and five-year-olds are not. Piaget's experiments showed the usual age for the development of this concept to be about seven, and that it was preceded by a transitional period of partial development.

96

Among the children I played this game with, those in the transitional stage tended to hesitate and say things like, "This one is fatter," or "It's got more room to spread out." One little boy, after pondering awhile, said, "Pour it back in the first glass and let me see it again."

game eighteen

Purpose: To let you know if your child has reached the stage of mental development where he is a conserver of discontinuous quantities.

Materials: Two identical glasses or glass jars.
A supply of small objects all alike and roughly uniform in size, such as beads, uncracked nuts, cranberries, dried beans, etc.
A shallow bowl.

Set the two glasses side by side, near the pile of nuts, beans, or whatever you are using.
"Take a nut in each hand. Put one in each glass at the same time." If your child can't manage this two-handed operation, put a nut in one glass yourself as he puts one in the other. Continue until the glasses are about 1/2 to 3/4 full. If the objects are irregularly shaped, shake the glasses to settle them into place.
"Does one glass have more nuts than the other?"
Most children will say there are the same in both. (If your child does not, start over and put fewer nuts in the glasses.)
Now pour the nuts out of one glass into the bowl.
"Do you think there are more nuts in the glass, or more in the bowl, or are they the same?"
Nonconservers will say there are more nuts in one. This is usually true of four- and five-year-olds.
They are misled by appearances, even though they themselves filled the glasses by a method of one-to-one correspondence that guarantees the same number in each.

Comments: This test is a bridge between the conservation of quantity and the conservation of number because the objects used can be counted, which is not true of a similar test with liquids.

A child does not necessarily develop the various kinds of conservation all at the same time. Several validation studies of Piaget's original experiments brought out the fact that some of these conservation tasks are easier for children than others. For example, conservation of discontinuous quantities (such as the objects used in this game) is apt to come at an earlier age than conservation of continuous quantities, such as liquids.

game nineteen

Purpose: To let you know if your child has reached the stage of mental development where he is a conserver of number. (See Chapter 2.)

Materials: Five cups.
A stack of six or seven saucers.

"Are there enough saucers in this stack so there will be one for each cup?" Suggest that he put a saucer under each cup to see, if he doesn't do this spontaneously. Do not rely on counting. The fact that he may count five cups and five saucers does not guarantee that he understands they are the same.
Remove the extra saucers. "Are there the same number of cups and saucers?"
Line the saucers up in a row, but take the cups out and bunch them together. "Do you think there are more cups, more saucers, or the same number?"
If he says there are more of one, suggest that he check by putting a cup in each saucer again.
Repeat the last question, but this time have the cups in a row and the saucers stacked up.

Comments: Do not be surprised if your child is not yet a conserver of number, even though he can count. Typically, he will progress from no conservation through a period of indecision, when he vacillates between thinking the number changes and thinking it doesn't, to a firm conviction that the number stays the same. If you ask him how he knows, a conserver will often say something like, "Because the cups were in the saucers before." Conservation usually comes as the child enters the stage of concrete operations.

game twenty

Purpose: To provide experience in one-to-one correspondence, which precedes counting.

Materials: About one and one-half dozen flat objects such as bottle caps, chips, or large buttons, approximately uniform in size and shape.

Arrange five buttons in a row, spacing them about one inch apart. Put the rest in a pile beside your child. "Can you make a row that will have the same number of buttons as mine?"
Younger children tend to make a row the same length as yours but with the buttons crowded closer together or spread farther apart so that they have the wrong number. They don't take into account the spaces between the buttons, but see only the overall configuration, as in the diagram on the facing page. At the next higher level of development they will often spontaneously place a button opposite each of yours—a one-to-one correspondence that automatically produces a row with the right number. If necessary, suggest this method.
Repeat several times, changing the number in your row.

Comments: Piaget's research into children's thinking about number revealed three characteristic phases of development. Younger than five, they believe the number of objects in two rows is equal if the rows are the same length. At five and a half to six, on the average, they think the number of objects are equal as long as the two rows are placed in one-to-one correspondence, but lose this belief as soon as one row is spread out. Around six and a half or seven, they can hang on to their belief no matter how the rows are rearranged.

(The ability to count was surprisingly little help in establishing equality of the rows if they looked different.)

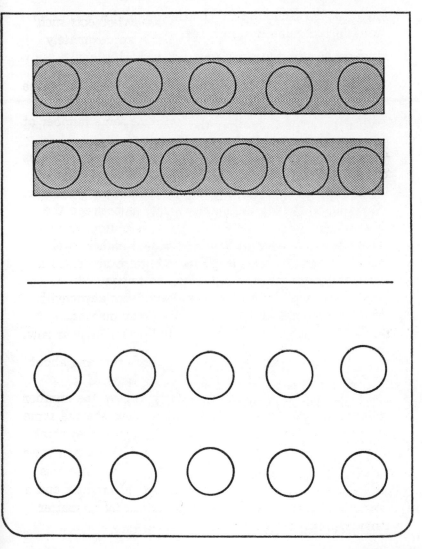

game twenty-one

Purpose: To provide a further test for (and experience with) conservation of number.

Materials: The same objects (bottle caps, chips, or buttons) used in the game on page 102.

Lay out five buttons in a row. Let your child make a row with an equal number by the method of one-to-one correspondence.

Remove the buttons that are left over.

When he is positive that the two rows have the same number, rearrange the buttons in your row into a group of three and a group of two.

"Do we both have the same number of buttons now?"
If he says No, start over, using fewer buttons. If he says Yes, suggest that he move one of his buttons away from the others.

"Do you think we still have the same number?" If he says Yes again, repeat, using more buttons in the original rows, separating them into groups any way you like as long as his and yours are different. Vary the questions—"Do you have more buttons than I do?" "Why do you think so?" "Does one of us have more buttons?" "Which one?" and so on.

At any answer that indicates he thinks the number has changed, suggest that he put the buttons back into the two rows opposite each other. If this doesn't work, start over, using fewer buttons.

Comments: In the transitional stage, children may simply answer, "I don't know." One little girl I played this game with said consistently that there were more buttons when the row was rearranged, but afterward would ask me, "Are there *really* more?" She was beginning to sense a difference between appearance and reality.

Piaget, in work done within the last ten years or so, found that children become conservers of number gradually, starting with small numbers and then developing the concept for larger and larger numerical sets. They might be conservers in the case of numbers up to ten, but nonconservers beyond that even though they could count much higher. (See Chapter 3.)

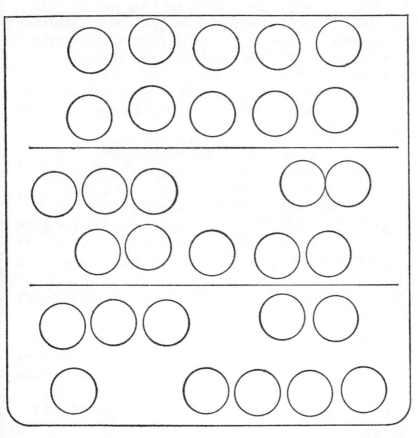

game twenty-two

Purpose: To provide further experience in thinking about number.

Materials: The same objects (bottle caps, chips, or buttons) used in the game on page 102.

Divide the buttons into two noticeably unequal piles.
"Which pile do you think has more buttons?"
Let your child take one button from each pile simultaneously, using both hands. Continue about six times, placing the buttons in two new piles. (Don't count.)
"Does one of the new piles have more buttons than the other new pile?"
If he thinks that it does, encourage him to find out by lining them up in two rows opposite each other (one-to-one correspondence).

Comments: Piaget's associate, Bärbel Inhelder, found that young children tend to think the new pile formed of objects drawn from the larger of the two original piles has more objects in it than the other new pile. They think the characteristic "more" carries over into the new pile, even though they themselves built the two new piles by a method that made them equal.

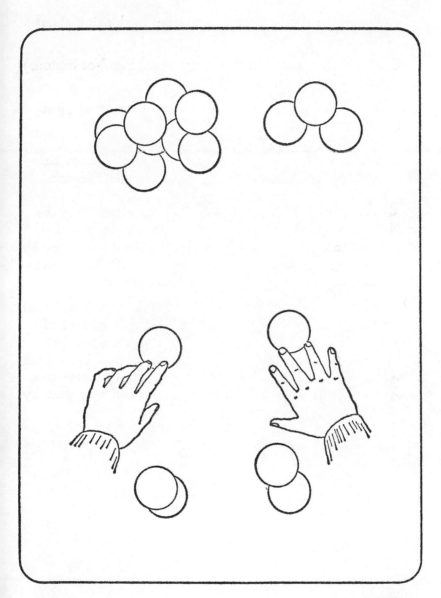

More Difficult Games

game one

Purpose: To provide experience in classification by two characteristics (color and shape) at one time.

Materials: The set of eighteen colored cards.

Take four squares, four circles, and four triangles, making sure that you have each shape in four different colors. Let your child sort them by shape. Put the triangles and the circles in two rows as shown in the diagram, but with the colors mixed.
"Can you fix them so red is under red, yellow under yellow, and so on all the way across?"
Add the row of squares (also with the colors mixed).
"Fix the squares, too, so the colors match."
When the cards are all arranged, start to play.
"Hide your eyes while I take one of the cards away." Keep the one you took concealed.
"Can you guess which card is missing?"
Repeat several times; then reverse roles and hide your eyes while the child removes a card. Now you guess which one is missing. (Don't be too good at it.)

Comments: In playing the guessing game, be sure to begin each time with the full arrangement so that only one card is missing at a time.
The child should identify the missing card by its two characteristics—"the red circle," for example.
If this game is easy for your child, make it more challenging by mixing the cards up before you take one away. Can he guess what card you took? Does it occur to him to arrange the cards as before, so that it is easy to tell what is missing?

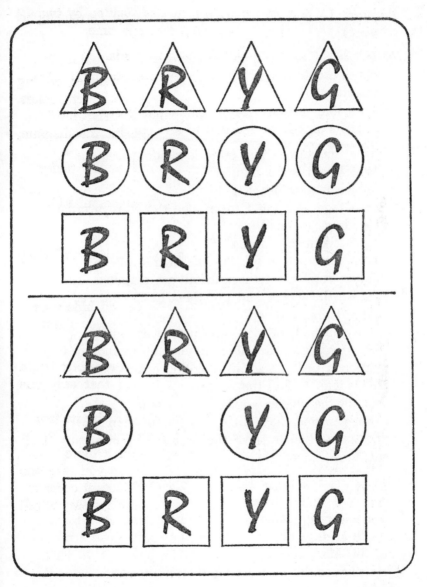

game two

Purpose: To provide experience in seriation (arranging in order).

Materials: Set of four measuring spoons graduated in size. (They usually range from 1/4 teaspoon to one tablespoon.)
Set of four measuring cups graduated in size. (They usually range from 1/4 cup to one cup.)

Place the cups on the table in random fashion.
"Which cup is the biggest?"
"Which is next biggest?"
Encourage your child to arrange the cups in order from large to small.
Repeat with the spoons.
"Let's match them up. Put the biggest spoon in the biggest cup." Continue until all are matched. Then remove the spoons and put them in the ordered row again. Point to a cup.
"Can you find the right spoon for this cup?"
Repeat, skipping around from one cup to another in no particular order. Vary by pointing to a spoon and asking him to find the right cup.
Mix all the objects up. Point to a cup.
"Can you find the right spoon for this cup now?"
Encourage him to solve the problem by arranging them all in order again.

Comments: You might think a problem involving double seriation would be harder than a single seriation, but Piaget's experiments did not turn out that way. If a child could arrange objects in order, he could solve a problem of this kind. Piaget's four-year-olds could not. At about six they could, by a trial-and-error process.

If this game is easy for your child, you can make it more challenging by having the spoons arranged in opposite order from the cups (small to large for one—large to small for the other). Point to the third cup and ask him to find the right spoon for it.

game three

Purpose: To provide experience in seriation (arranging in order).

Materials: Six drinking straws.

Leave one straw full length. Cut one inch off the second, two inches off the third, three inches off the fourth, and so on, so that you have six straws graduated in length. Mix them up and place on the table.
"Can you fix these in stairsteps?"
Be sure he puts one end of each straw against something straight, like the edge of the table. Children are apt to look only at the end of the straw that is making the stairstep, and let the other end stick out irregularly, which would mean that the straws weren't really arranged in order of length.
"Which is the longest straw? Which is the shortest? Which is next to the longest?"

Comments: Notice whether your child uses trial and error in arranging the straws in stairsteps—starting by measuring any two straws against each other, then others picked at random, and so on—or if he goes about it systematically by finding the longest (or shortest) straw first and working methodically from there. A trial-and-error method is characteristic of the preoperational stage of mental development (see Chapter 2), a systematic method is characteristic of the concrete operational stage.

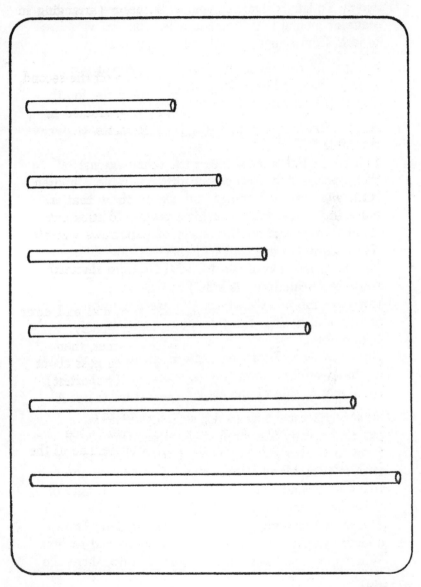

game four

Purpose: To let you know if your child has reached the stage of mental development where he can visualize objects from someone else's viewpoint.

Materials: A rectangular box, such as a cereal box.
A large ball or blown-up balloon.
Pencil (or crayon) and paper.

Arrange the box and ball side by side in the center of the table.
Seat your child on one side of the table and yourself on the opposite side, facing each other.
"Can you draw the things you see on the table?" Do not criticize the quality of his drawing. When he has finished, give him another sheet of paper.
"Now draw the box and ball the way you think they look from my side of the table." (He must do this while still seated on his side.)
Compare the two drawings. We are not testing his artistic ability—it is the placement of the objects that is important.
Does the second drawing show them in reverse order, as they would be from the viewpoint of the person on the opposite side of the table?

Comments: Most five-year-olds will make the second drawing exactly like the first—both showing the objects from their own point of view. I tried this experiment with forty children, aged five and a half to six, and only two had second drawings that were correct. One of these had done it by turning his paper upside down (whether accidentally or on purpose, I don't know) and drawing the box and ball as they looked to him. When the paper was turned right side up, there the objects were, seen from the opposite viewpoint. Piaget's experiment in which he asked the children to visualize a model of three mountains as seen from other positions (see Chapter 2) showed that this ability was partially developed at seven or eight, but on the average not fully so until nine or ten.

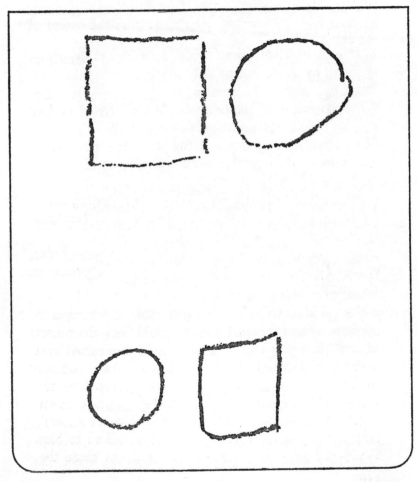

game five

Purpose: To let you know if your child has reached the stage of mental development where he can visualize objects from a viewpoint different from his own.

Materials: Pencil or crayon.
Paper.
A square or rectangular table, bare on top. (A card table is ideal.)

Seat your child across the room from the table, which is going to serve as a model for his drawing. Let him draw the table as he sees it.
"How do you think the table would look if you were up on the ceiling looking right down at it?"
"Can you draw a picture of the table to show me the way you think it would look from up there?"

Comments: It is rare for preschool-age children to be able to do this. Usually their second drawing is just like their first, legs and all. Some children realize that the legs wouldn't show from above, but they still may draw a side view of the table top as seen edge on, like the first drawing in the diagram on page 120. The majority of first graders can't do this, either. However, a class of six-year-olds in a British Infant School could all draw a table correctly as it would be seen from above. They had had a great deal of experience in making models from cardboard boxes, which seemed to have given them a feel for shapes seen from various angles. The illustrations in the two diagrams are not to be taken as models, but are shown just to give you an idea how preschoolers' drawings of tables often look. It is quite all right if your child's drawing is not like

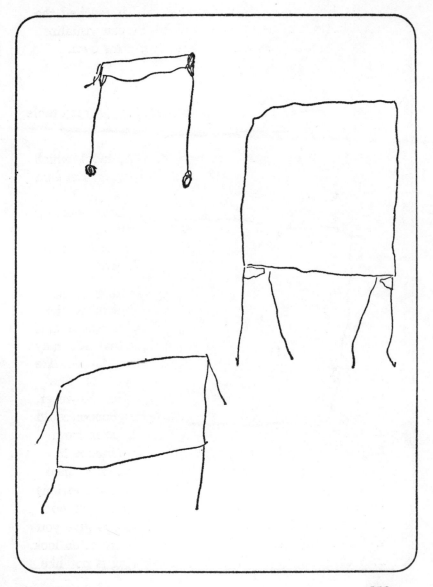

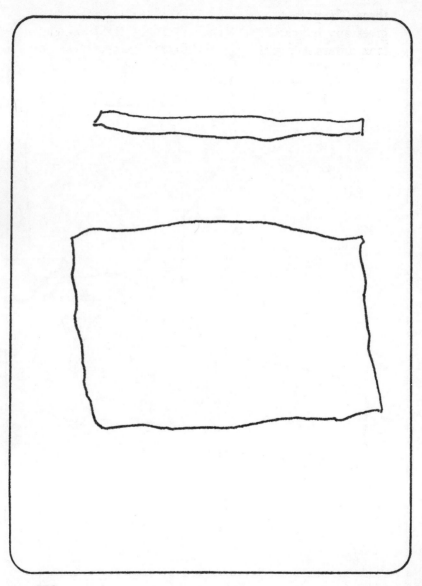

these. The point to notice is whether his second drawing gives any indication that he realizes the table would look different if seen from a different viewpoint.

game six

Purpose: To provide experience in discovering simple patterns.

Materials: The set of eighteen colored cards.

Spread out the cards on the table. In a clear place line up a blue square, then a blue triangle, followed by a yellow square and a yellow triangle, as in the diagram. "What card do you think should come next?"
After the child has found a square and put it in place, ask, "What comes next after that?" (Note that the square and the following triangle are the same color.)
Repeat with other simple patterns, such as those suggested in the diagram.
Reverse roles. Let your child invent a pattern of his own and see if you can guess what card would come next.

Comments: This is hard for a great many children. Often they don't discover your pattern but extend the row according to some idea of their own. If your child wants to do this, let him. Look for some recurring pattern (even an accidental one) in the cards he lines up and go on from there.
Recognition of patterns and relationships is an important part of analytical ability. A child's success in the use of patterns will help to guide his thinking in the future. Those who have seen and used patterns previously are more alert to patterns that exist within a problem.

[B] △B [Y] △Y ? ?

[R] [Y] [B] [R] ? ?

(G) [R] [R] (B) [Y] ?

game seven

Purpose: To provide experience in seriation (arranging in order).

Materials: A package of construction paper or heavy brown wrapping paper. (Old Christmas wrappings are fine.) Child's scissors (round-ended).
Pencils.

This works best if several people of different sizes are available—father, mother, preschooler, brother and/or sister and/or a playmate or two.
Each person draws around one foot (shoe and all) of the person next to him.
Let the children cut the patterns out, and you write the identifying name on each.
"Who has the biggest foot?"
"Which one is next biggest?"
"Who has the smallest?"
Continue until the feet are all arranged in order of size.

Comments: If you have a bulletin board at home, the paper feet can be thumbtacked to it in order. From time to time visitors' feet may be added to the collection, each one fitted into place according to size. (I don't think your bridge club is going to like this.)

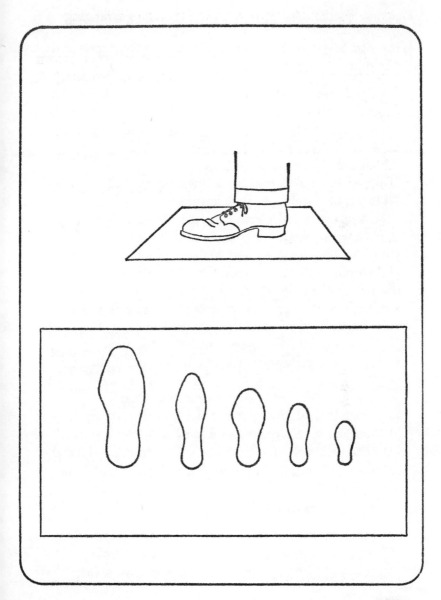

game eight

Purpose: To provide further experience with patterns.

Materials: Sixteen of the colored cards. (Omit one red circle and one red triangle.)

Give your child all the red and green cards. Keep the yellow and blue ones for yourself. Arrange your cards in the pattern shown at the top left of the diagram. Point to the yellow circle.

"What color and shape is this?"

"Do you have a yellow circle in your cards?"

"What color circles do you have?"

"You can use a red circle in place of my yellow one."

Repeat with your blue triangle and his green triangle, your two blue squares and his two green squares, and so on, until he has built up the pattern shown at the top right of the diagram. Help him to see that his reds represent your yellows and his greens represent your blues.

"Let's take the cards apart and build the man again."

Arrange your yellows and blues in the same pattern as before.

"Can you make yours by yourself this time?"

In a variation of this game, build the pattern shown in the diagram on page 128 a card at a time, starting with the yellow square that has a blue triangle stacked on top of it. Suggest that your child follow with his, card for card.

"Can you guess what we're making?"

Comments: Mathematicians call this "mapping." Each object of one set represents a corresponding (but not identical) object in another set, as a dot on a map

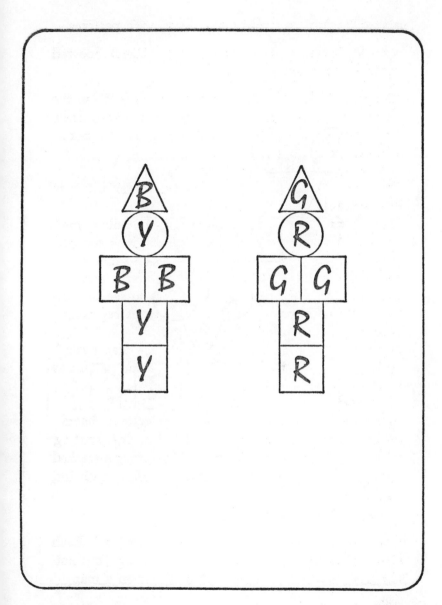

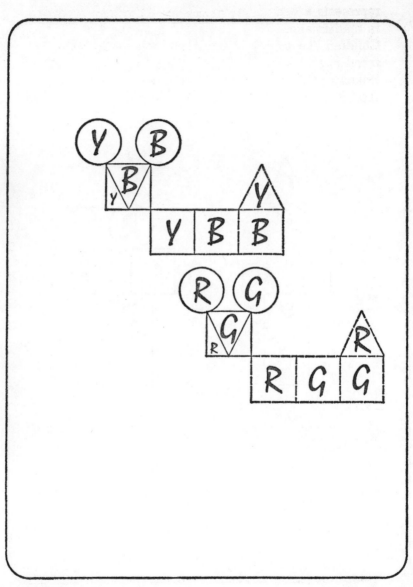

represents a certain town. It is an important concept in mathematics.

Children like to talk about what they are making. I asked one little girl if she thought the first pattern looked like anything. She said, "Yes. A man with one leg." Another said, "A clown."

game nine

Purpose: To provide experience in classification by either color or shape.

Materials: The whole set of eighteen colored cards.
A white string about one yard long.
Two small pieces of colorless Scotch Tape.

Divide the tabletop in two parts by laying the string down the middle, taping it at each end. Place a blue circle and a blue square on one side of the table. "These two go together because they are alike in one way." Give the child all the rest of the cards. "Can you find one card that is like both of these?" When he has found one, let him place it beside the two blue cards already on the table. "Put all the cards that go with these on this side of the table. Put all the cards that are different from these on the other side of the table." Vary the game by starting with two cards that are alike in shape, for example, a red circle and a green circle. Trade roles, and let the child put out the first two cards while you deduce how they are alike.

Comments: Give your child plenty of time to think— sometimes you can almost see the wheels go around. It may take him several trials to get the solution. If he is stuck, ask, "How are these two alike?" Emphasize that he is looking for one card that is like both these. If he needs a hint you can tell him, "They are both blue."

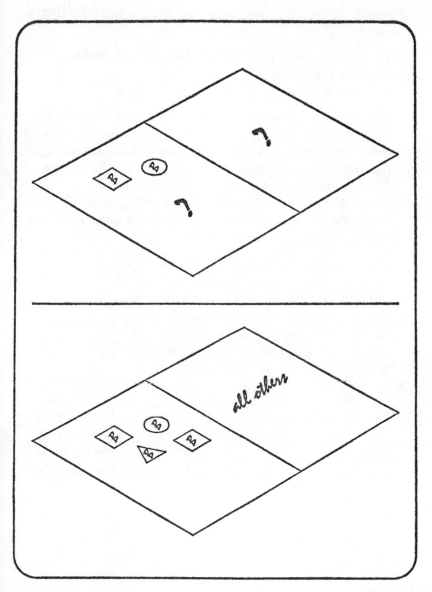

game ten

Purpose: To provide experience in classification by either color or shape.

Materials: The whole set of eighteen colored cards.
A white string about one yard long.
Two small pieces of colorless Scotch Tape.

Divide the tabletop as you did before.
Place the yellow triangle on one side of the table, pick up the yellow circle, and say, "This card is different, so I will put it on the other side of the table."
Give the child all the other cards.
Point to the yellow triangle, and say, "Can you put all the cards that are like this one with it? Put all the cards that are different on the other side of the table."

Comments: This problem is harder than the one on the preceding page. Many children overlook the information given by the yellow circle. The yellow triangle tells them that a matching card can either be yellow or it can be a triangle. The presence of the yellow circle on the *other* side of the table rules out the first possibility.
If he needs help, ask, "How are the two cards different?"

game eleven

Purpose: To provide experience in classification by either color or shape.

Materials: The whole set of eighteen colored cards.
An empty box or basket of a convenient size to hold the cards.
A small towel or scarf to cover the box.

Give five cards in assorted colors and shapes to the child, and five to yourself. For example, the child might have one red square, one blue square, one green triangle, one yellow triangle, and one red circle. You might have one green square, one yellow square, one red triangle, one blue triangle, and one blue circle. Put the rest of the cards in the box and cover it with the cloth.
To start play, reach into the box without looking under the cover, and draw one card. Lay it on the table between you and the child. Suppose it is the green circle. He can play a card that matches it either in color or in shape. Continue alternately in this way. If either player has no matching card to play, he draws from the covered box until he gets one. Any cards that he draws that do not match must be added to his hand.
Whoever first plays all the cards in his hand is the winner.

Comments: Let your child win at least half the time—maybe oftener. If he has not reached the age when he enjoys competitive games like this, don't press him. Come back to this game when he is a little older.

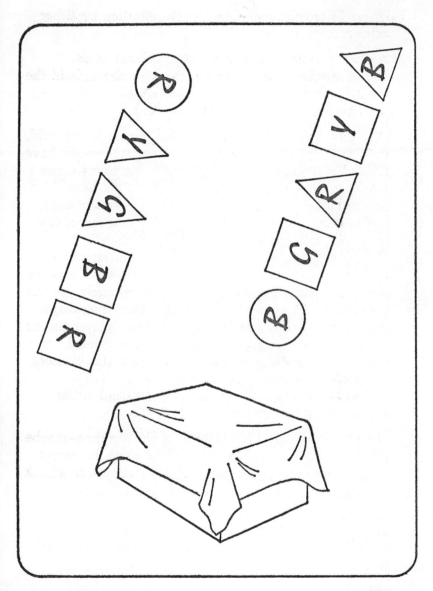

game twelve

Purpose: To provide experience in classification involving subclasses.

Materials: A magnet. (Some potholders have a small magnet stitched inside that can be easily ripped out. Or you can get a toy horseshoe-shaped magnet at the dime store for less than a quarter.)
An empty egg carton.
A piece of string.
About two dozen assorted objects chosen from the following list (be sure you include some of the ones that a magnet will not attract):

Paper clips	Buttons
Safety pins (closed)	Bottle caps
Bobby pins	Beads
Hair clips	

Put the objects in a deep box or other receptacle. (A half-gallon milk carton works well.) Tie a long-enough string to the magnet to reach the bottom of the box. Let your child use the magnet to fish in the box, and put his catch in the egg carton—paper clips in one cavity, safety pins in another, and so on. The objects that a magnet will not attract are left in the bottom of the "pond." When he has finished, ask, "What's the difference between the things in the egg carton and those left in the box?"

Comments: The two major classes are determined by the single attribute of magnetic attraction. One of them is then separated into subclasses according to other characteristics. The game will vary in complexity, depending on the objects used. For example, some safety pins are made of metal that a magnet will pick up;

some aren't. If they are mixed, both major classes contain some safety pins. The same is true of covered buttons that have a metal core.

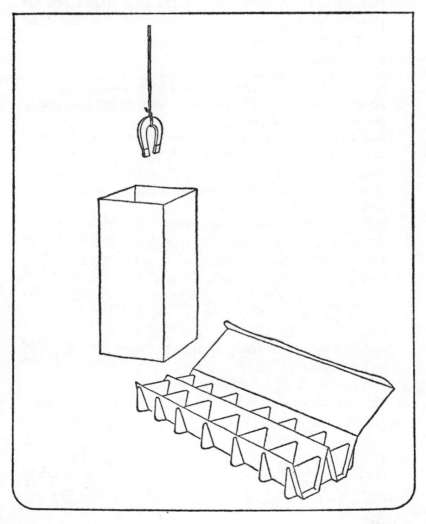

game thirteen

Purpose: To provide experience in seriation.

Materials: Magnet, string, and deep box used in game on
  page 136.
  Colored paper (old Christmas wrappings work well).
  Four paper clips.
  A piece of cardboard about 1 foot by 1 foot.
  Scotch Tape.

Cut the paper into eight strips 3/4 inch wide, making one
10 inches long, one 9 inches long, one 8 inches long, etc.,
on down to 3 inches.
Roll the 9-inch strip up and fasten with a paper clip. Do
the same with the 7-, the 5-, and the 3-inch strips.
Tape the remaining strips to the cardboard in order of
length, as shown in the diagram, leaving about one
inch of space between each strip.
Put the rolled, paper-clipped strips into a deep box.
At the start of the game, show your child the cardboard,
and let him use the magnet to fish another strip out of the
box. After it is unrolled, ask, "Where do you think this
one fits in the stairsteps?" Encourage him to find out by
comparing lengths. When he has decided, help him to
tape the strip into place (even if it's the wrong place).
Repeat until all the strips have been fished out and taped
to the cardboard.
"Do you think these stairsteps are in the right order?"
Let him change any he wants to.

Comments: Piaget found that inserting new objects into
  a series that was already constructed was just as difficult
  for children as arranging a whole series from scratch.
  Don't use paper with a decided pattern, such as Santa
  Clauses, which often cause children to try to match the

pattern on the strips instead of concentrating
on the length.
If your child wants to put the rolled up strip back in the
box and fish it out again, instead of unrolling it right then,
that's all right.

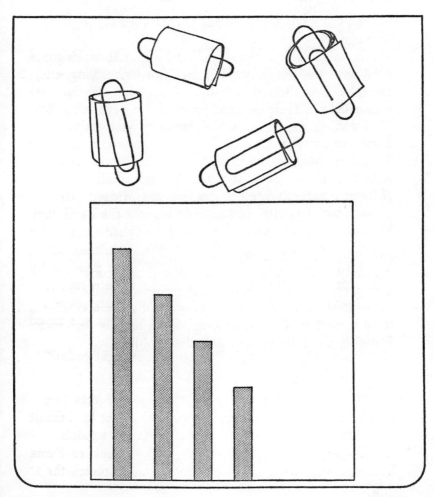

game fourteen

Purpose: To provide experience in recognizing linear order.

Materials: Three spools of thread in three distinctive colors. Cardboard tube from the center of a roll of paper towels. A piece of string about a yard long.

Thread the spools on the string as described in the game on page 74.
While your child watches, pull the string through the tube until the spools are hidden from sight. Now rotate the tube itself through a half circle, so that the ends are reversed from their original positions.
"If I pull on the string, which spool do you think will come out first?"
"Pull the string and see."
Repeat, rotating the tube through a full circle this time. If he can correctly predict the first spool in both these cases, continue with various combinations of full- and half-circle turns of the tube.

Comments: This is a harder variation of the game on page 74, and is suitable for more advanced children. The younger ones usually realize that the spools will come out of the tube in the same order they went in, which suffices for a correct prediction as long as the tube is stationary. Rotating the tube complicates the problem.

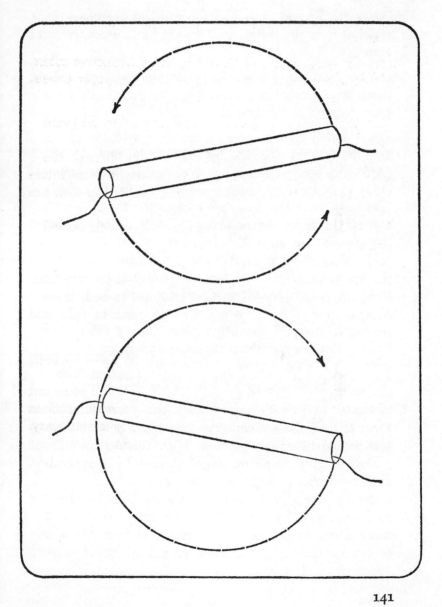

game fifteen

Purpose: To let you know if your child has reached the
stage of mental development where he is a conserver of
area.

Materials: Two equal-size pieces of thin cardboard, about
seven or eight inches square. (Empty cereal boxes are
good sources of cardboard.)

Draw dotted lines on one square similar to the figure.
Lay the two squares side by side on the table.
"Are these squares the same size?" (Encourage your
child to find out by putting one on top of the other.)
"Do they cover the same amount of the table?"
Cut off the upper corner along the dotted line and move
the piece as shown in the diagram.
"Now, does this figure cover the same amount of table as
the whole square?" If he says No, suggest that he put
the piece back where it was and compare the two
squares.
Repeat, cutting off the other pieces along the dotted
lines and arranging them in more and more complex
ways.
"Can you fit all the pieces back together?"

Comments: In Piaget's experiments the younger children
(four to five) did not conserve area when part of a figure
was moved to a new location. Then came a transitional
period of gradual awareness, followed by conservation
at about seven to eight years of age.
A ready-made jigsaw puzzle can be substituted for the
cardboard one, if you turn it over so the picture doesn't
show. Draw an outline of the outside edge of the puzzle
to use for comparison of area, as the second cardboard
square is used above.

142

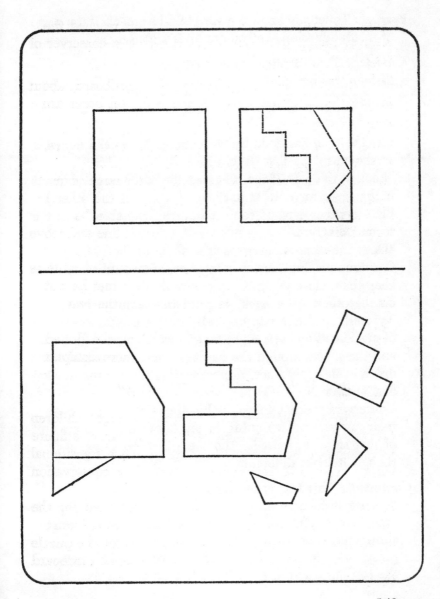

game sixteen

Purpose: To let you know if your child has reached the stage of mental development where he is a conserver of area.

Materials: Two identical table mats.
Sixteen playing cards.

Place one mat on top of the other. "Are these the same size?"
Lay the two mats side by side and place a card on each, as shown in the first diagram.
"Look at the part of the mat that the cards don't cover. Is it the same for both mats?"
Place another card on each mat, arranging them as in the second diagram.
"Does the same amount of mat show on both?"
Continue placing the cards in pairs, one to each mat, but keep them close together on one mat and scattered out on the other. After each pair ask the same question.
Typically, children will begin by saying the same amount of mat shows on both. As more and more cards are placed and the spaces around the cards become increasingly different in appearance, nonconservers fall for the illusion and answer No.
Conservers are not taken in by appearances, but base their answers on reasoning. They know that the amount of mat showing must be the same in both cases, even though it looks different.

Comments: This test is harder than the preceding one because it focuses on complementary area (that is, the area that is left) when larger and larger portions are subtracted from the original. Don't expect your preschooler to have developed this concept. However, the test has a sort of built-in scale with eight steps. The point at which he switches from Yes to No gives a clue about his progress toward conservation.

game seventeen

Purpose: To provide experience in seriation.

Materials: Paper and pencil.

Copy the drawings of the telephone pole shown on the facing page, using a separate piece of paper for each one. Shuffle the pieces of paper around and lay them on the table.

Point out the one showing the upright pole to your child.

"This is a telephone pole that got knocked over. These other pictures show it falling down. Can you put them in order?"

If he has difficulty, stand the pencil up on the table and slowly tip it over while he watches.

Comments: This is often hard for children in the four-to-seven age bracket. They tend to focus on the first and the final states of any transformation, and ignore the sequence of steps in between.

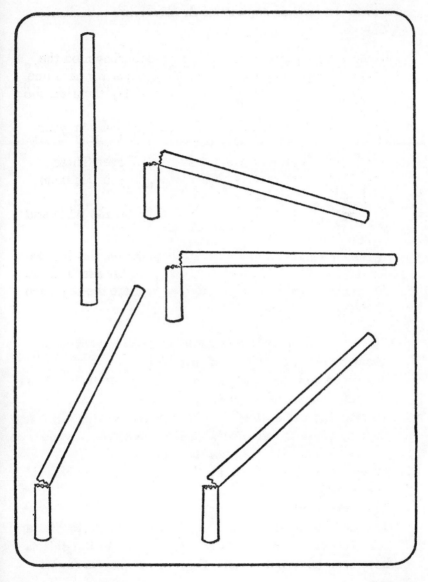

147

game eighteen

Purpose: To provide experience in classifying miscellaneous objects.

Materials: About two dozen items similar to the following (make sure that each item is different and that there are an even number of items):

A small piece of aluminum foil	A button
A pencil	A piece of soap
A paper clip	A hair clip
A spool	A clothes pin
A sponge	A marble
A bottle cap	A small comb
An unshelled nut	A wad of cotton
A bobby pin	A pebble
A rubber band	A belt buckle
An eraser	An old toothbrush
An emery board	A safety pin
A spoon	A bead

Spread the objects out on a table and talk to your child about them. Encourage him to find new ways of describing and classifying them in addition to the familiar ones of color, shape, and size.

To start the game, the first player picks up two objects, saying, "These are alike because . . ." and gives a valid reason, such as: They're both red, both round, both fasten clothes, both scratchy, both shiny, and so on. He puts the two objects in front of him.

The second player does the same.

The game continues until one player is unable to find a pair that have a common attribute or until all the objects have been taken out of play. Each of the players counts

148

the objects in his pile, and the one with the most is the winner.

Comments: Vary the items according to whether your child is a boy or a girl. Introduce some new objects into the game when you repeat it, including a few that are novel to the child. The level of sophistication of the game depends on the objects used.
Skill in comparing and classifying objects is important in the study of science. Such skill is built up from two factors—observation of the objects (which includes not only looking but also handling, squeezing, poking, and so on) and the ability to draw conclusions from what has been observed.

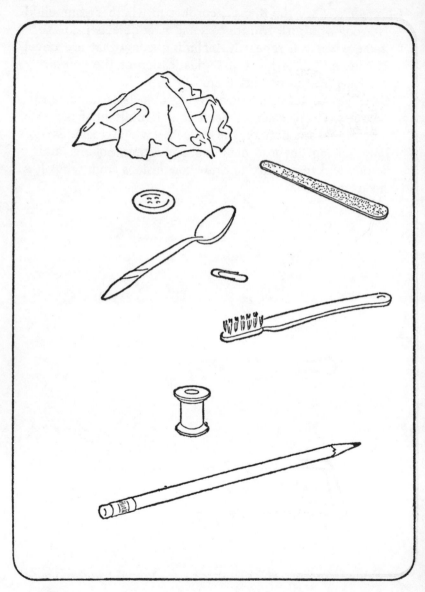

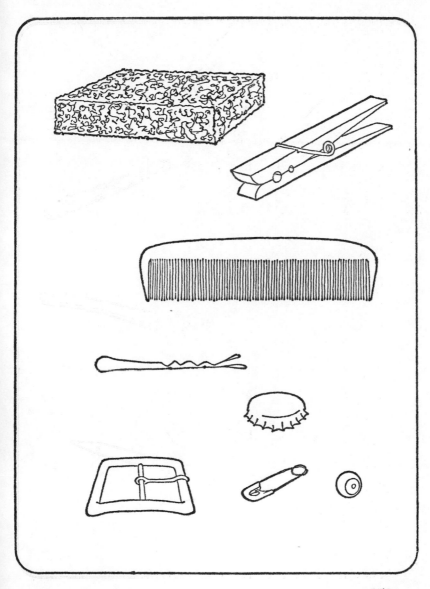

bibliography

Bruner, Jerome S. *The Process of Education.* Cambridge, Mass.:
Harvard University Press, 1960.
——, *Toward a Theory of Instruction.* Cambridge, Mass.: The
Belknap Press of Harvard University Press, 1966.
——, Rose R. Olver, Patricia M. Greenfield, *et al. Studies in Cog-
nitive Growth.* New York: Wiley and Sons, Inc., 1966.
Flavell, John H. *The Developmental Psychology of Jean Piaget.*
Princeton, N.J.: D. Van Nostrand Company, Inc., 1963.
Hunt, J. McVicker. *Intelligence and Experience.* New York: The
Ronald Press Company, 1961.
Karplus, Robert. "Theoretical Background of the Science Curricu-
lum Improvement Study," *Journal of Research in Science
Teaching,* October, 1965.
Klausmeier, Herbert J., and Chester W. Harris. *Analyses of Con-
cept Learning.* New York: Academic Press, 1966.
Piaget, Jean. *The Child's Conception of Number.* New York: Hu-
manities, 1952.

Piaget, Jean. "How Children Form Mathematical Concepts," *Scientific American*, November, 1953.

——. *Logic and Psychology*. New York: Basic Books, Inc., 1957.

——, and Bärbel Inhelder. *La Genèse des Structures Logiques Élémentaires: Classifications et Sériations*. Neuchâtel: Delachaux et Niestle, 1959.

Pines, Maya. *Revolution in Learning*. New York: Harper & Row, 1967.

The Schools Council. *Mathematics in Primary Schools: Curriculum Bulletin No. 1*. London: Her Majesty's Stationery Office, 1966.

Suppes, Patrick. "Mathematical Concept Formation in Children," *American Psychologist*, February, 1966.

——. "Tomorrow's Education?" *Education Age*, January-February, 1966.

——. "The Case for Information-Oriented (Basic) Research in Mathematics Education," in J. M. Scandura (Ed.), *Research in Mathematics Education*, Washington, D.C., 1967.

——. "The Psychological Foundations of Mathematics," *Colloques Internationaux du Centre National de la Recherche Scientifique*. Paris: Editions de Centre National de la Recherche Scientifique, 1967.

——, and Irene Rosenthal-Hill. *Concept Formation by Kindergarten Children in a Card-Sorting Task*. Psychology Series, Stanford University, Stanford, California, 1967.

Yeomans, Edward. *Education for Initiative and Responsibility. Comments on a Visit to the Schools of Leicestershire County*. Boston: National Association of Independent Schools, 1967.

index

M